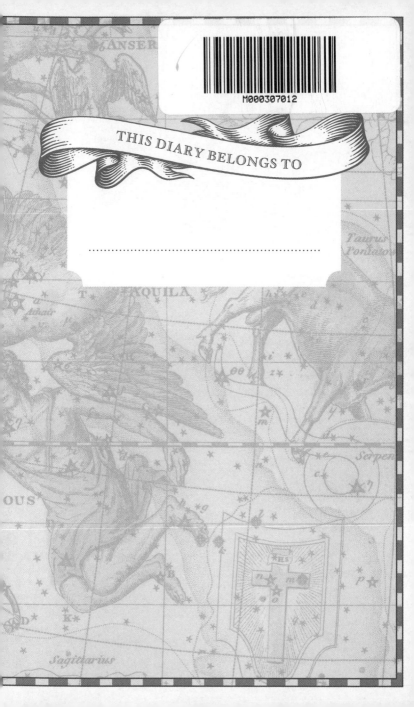

THIS DIARY BELONGS TO

....

2023
Astrology Diary

Patsy Bennett

ROCKPOOL

A Rockpool book
PO Box 252
Summer Hill
NSW 2130
Australia

rockpoolpublishing.com
Follow us! **f** 🄌 rockpoolpublishing
Tag your images with #rockpoolpublishing

ISBN: 9781922579096
Northern hemisphere edition

Published in 2022, by Rockpool Publishing
Copyright text © Patsy Bennett, 2022
Copyright design © Rockpool Publishing 2022

Internal design by Jessica Le, Rockpool Publishing
Cover design and typsetting by Sara Lindberg, Rockpool Publishing
Edited by Lisa Macken

Frontispiece by W.G. Evans, 1856, Map of the Constellations in July, August, September.
Other map illustrations by Alexander Jamieson, 1822, Celestial Atlas.
Glyph illustrations by http://All-Silhouettes.com
Zodiac illustrations by http://vectorian.net
Compass illustration by Jessica Le, Rockpool Publishing

Printed and bound in China
10 9 8 7 6 5 4 3 2 1

NB: the planetary phenomena and aspects listed on each day are set to
Greenwich Mean Time (GMT) apart from the summer time (26 March
to 29 October), where they are set to British Summer Time. To convert
times to your location please see www.timeanddate.com. Astrological
interpretations take into account all aspects and the sign the sun and
planets are in on each day and are not taken out of context.

introduction

Make 2023 your best year yet! This is the year to start something new. It is also a year of considerable socio-economic change, so it's a good time to adapt to the zeitgeist. Be practical and grounded while also being open minded, as this will help you to flourish in this transformational climate.

This diary/planner is designed to help you to make the most of your year. If you live your life by the sun, moon and stars you'll love the *2023 Astrology Diary*: you'll have expert astrological advice right at your fingertips! I have interpreted major daily astrological data in the diary pages to help you plan ahead so that 2023 will be all you wish it to be. Simply follow the diary dates, and the interpretations of astrological phenomena will help you to plan ahead and enjoy your days. (Please see 'How to use this diary' for more details about the terminology used in the diary pages.)

The major strategies for personal growth and success this year are:

- adapt to the zeitgeist
- build a strong foundation that will enable you to grow
- be kind to yourself and others
- be innovative, creative and imaginative
- start something new
- be practical and grounded
- find ways to manage anger and frustration.

The major planetary transit in 2023 will be the transit of Pluto into the sign of Aquarius. Pluto is an agent of change on a big-picture level, and as it leaves Capricorn and steps into Aquarius it will bring long-term transformation globally. Pluto changes signs on average once every 20 years, making this year's transit into Aquarius super relevant on a generational level.

When Pluto changes signs it historically signals major socio-economic change. The last time Pluto changed signs – from Sagittarius to Capricorn – was in 2008, when the global financial crash occurred. It was to be expected that finances would be a focus of deep transformation as Capricorn is the sign of established systems, and especially financial systems.

In 2023 Pluto will transit into Aquarius, the air sign of innovation and technology. Both Pluto and Aquarius concern themselves with the populace – that is, with transformation that affects humanity for the foreseeable future – so we can expect to see major changes regarding engineering, the digital world, robotics and space exploration. On a personal level, many people will be striving to adapt to new ideas and revolutionise their lives in some way.

In 2023 the transit of Pluto into Aquarius will only last from the end of March until mid-June, so the period from April until mid-June in 2023 will provide a taste of future developments as Pluto will subsequently remain in Aquarius from 2025 until 2044.

As Pluto in Aquarius is likely to put the spotlight on technology, manufacturing and the digital world, financially we can expect to see considerable developments concerning digital currencies in 2023.

On a social level, platforms such as social media and news outlets will enter the spotlight, continuing a trend that began in the late 2010s to delineate between fact-based news and fake news, key information and assumptions. And, because Aquarius rules innovation that affects the masses, we can expect serious and expansive developments and innovation in energy resources.

The month of May will be particularly important regarding all of the above. Pluto will form this year's second most important aspect: a trine (a 120-degree angle) with Uranus, the planet that rules Aquarius. This doubly strengthens the innovative aspect of the year, albeit with a retrograde Pluto signalling potential teething problems with long-term socio-economic change and innovation on all of the platforms mentioned.

Luckily, the trine aspect between Pluto and Uranus suggests that innovation and change will lead to a more enlightened future. This transit could bring out people's humanitarian qualities despite or even because of teething problems in developments. On the upside, the Pluto–Uranus trine will be the glue in the sandwich that cements in a positive way any perceived risk taking and the negatives of forays into fresh domains and massive socio-economic change. We will see there is solid potential and possibility in the future, as opposed to senseless destruction and endings.

The Pluto–Uranus trine aspect will be in force for most of the second half of the year. On a personal level, fresh projects and ideas may experience teething problems, but in recognising the obstacles progress can be made.

If you have innovative ideas for 2023, be prepared to invest in them. You may have quirky, brainstorm-type ideas, and they will be worth investigating at the very least. The first two months of 2023 are excellent for beginning new ventures, especially if you're an Aquarian, Leo,

Taurus or Scorpio. Ventures created at this time are most likely to take off, especially humanitarian and technological projects, whether they are instigated now or later in 2023 and early 2024.

Jupiter in Aries from the start of the year until mid-May adds to the picture that 2023 is the year to begin something new. Jupiter, the planet that rules abundance and good luck, will be a motivating force that encourages you to take steps into a fresh domain. Be brave but not foolhardy. A side note with Jupiter transits is to always avoid over-exuberance and exaggeration. Be realistic with finances and plans, or this transit could land you in hot water.

There will be no planets retrograde in the months of February or March and most of April, adding to the sense that the first quarter of the year is ideal for getting things done.

However, at mid-year pressures could lead to difficulties, both on a personal and a global level.

You must be prepared to embrace change, as a true pitfall in 2023 will be obstinacy and the inability to accept change. These two qualities will hold you back from venturing into a future that may be quite different from the one you envisage. The key quality to ensure it is the future you want is to embrace the spirit of humanitarianism.

Other true pitfalls in 2023 will be fanaticism and rebellion. Globally, there is likely to be a spirit of rebellion and intense fanaticism that could lead to conflict and war as pressures that have built up over past years find expression.

The year 2023 is the one to channel restless energy into something new, fulfilling, humanitarian and positive. Remember that starting something fresh necessitates building a strong platform from which to take a running leap into the new. Avoid destroying valid platforms and structures you've built in your life in the hope something better will materialise. It is, instead, the time to strategise and construct.

On 17 July the moon's north node enters Aries on the same day as there is a new moon in Cancer. The collective focus will be brought once again to a need to look for something new in life that is not only exciting and innovative but also nurturing. It also brings the focus back to personal responsibility for happiness and progress.

While the world turns and innovative ideas are seeded and take flight, it'll be important to ask how you can best express yourself through your plans and ideas and, above all, to take action so that your personal happiness and fulfilment become paramount. However, Aries is an antagonistic and warrior-like energy when expressed at its selfish worst, so care must be taken during the second half of the year to avoid conflict or it will escalate quickly – both in your personal life and globally.

The motto for 2023? *Be open minded, humanitarian and innovative.*

How to use this diary

Solar, lunar and planetary movements

This diary lists the major solar, planetary and lunar movements day by day, and I have interpreted these so you can plan your days, weeks and months according to prevailing astrological trends. You'll gain insight into which days will be favourable for your planned events – from important meetings, get-togethers and celebrations to trips and life decisions – and which days will be variable and may even be frustrating. You'll see when you plan your life by the stars that sometimes taking ill-timed action can lead to disappointment while taking well-timed action will lead to success.

The sun in the zodiac signs

Astrology is the study of the movement of celestial objects from our point of view here on earth. We are most familiar with the study of our sun signs, which depicts the movement and placement of the sun in the zodiac signs Aries through to Pisces. In the same way the sun moves through the zodiac signs Aries to Pisces through the calendar year, so too do the planets and other celestial objects such as the centaur Chiron.

    This diary features monthly forecasts when the sun is in each sign, beginning with the sun in Capricorn (December 2022 to January 2023) and proceeding through the signs and finishing once again with the sun in Capricorn in December 2023.

    Each monthly forecast applies to everyone, as it is a general forecast for all sun signs. There is also a forecast unique to your own particular sun sign; thus you'll find the 'For Capricorn' section is uniquely for Capricorns and so on. When the sun is in your own sign it can prove particularly motivational and is a great time to get ahead with projects that resonate with your self-esteem, gut instincts and bigger-picture motivation.

The moon in the zodiac signs

Just as the sun moves through the zodiac signs, so too does the moon. This diary lists these movements as they can have a perceived influence over the mood and tone of the day, just as the sun in different signs is known to characterise different traits. Where a diary entry states 'The moon enters Taurus' it indicates that the moon has left the zodiac sign Aries and entered the sign of Taurus, and will now reside in Taurus until it moves on to Gemini in a couple of days' time.

New moons and full moons are also listed in this diary, as these can mark turning points within your journey through the year. New moons are generally a great time to begin a fresh project. Full moons can signify a culmination or a peak in a project or event, so if you're planning to launch a business or your children wish to begin a new course or activity you can check in this diary if the day you're planning your event will be favourable for beginning a fresh venture. Simply check to see if your venture falls on or near a new moon, and also take a look at the diary entries either side of your proposed event to ensure celestial influences will be working in your favour.

Eclipses can indicate particularly powerful turning points, and it is for this reason eclipses are also listed in the diary dates. If a lunar or solar eclipse is in the same sign as your own sun sign it may be particularly potent.

The phases of the moon can truly influence the tone of your day, so this diary features every moon sign for every day. The moon remains in each sign for approximately two days. Listed below is the mood depending on which sign the moon is in on a daily basis.

MOON IN ARIES: can bring an upbeat approach to life, but restlessness or fiery outbursts can result if you or those around you feel they are under pressure.

MOON IN TAURUS: can bring stability to feelings and routine, a sensual time and predilection for all things artistic and musical, but overindulgence and stubbornness can result if you are under pressure.

MOON IN GEMINI: can bring a chatty, talkative approach to life, but flippancy, indecision and uncertainty can result if you or those around you feel under pressure.

MOON IN CANCER: a sense of security, nesting, cocooning and nurturance will be sought for family time and those you love, but insecurities or a lack of adaptability can result if you feel you are under pressure.

MOON IN LEO: an upbeat approach to life and more dynamic attitude to others and yourself will arise, but a Leo moon can bring arrogance, pride and vanity to the surface if you are under pressure.

MOON IN VIRGO: a great time to focus on health, routine, decluttering, work and being helpful, but overanalysis, obsessive attention to detail and ambivalence can also arise if you are under pressure.

MOON IN LIBRA: a lovely time to focus on art, music, love and creating harmony and peace, but a sense of disharmony, indecision and dissatisfaction can arise if you're under pressure.

MOON IN SCORPIO: a time for focusing on personal needs, sensuality, enjoyment of life and indulgence in all things wonderful, but if you are under pressure deep feelings that are intense or potentially destructive can emerge.

MOON IN SAGITTARIUS: an outgoing, upbeat phase when an adventurous attitude will bring out your joviality and lust for learning and life. If you're under pressure you and others may appear blunt or disregard the feelings of other people.

MOON IN CAPRICORN: can stimulate a practical and focused approach to work and to your goals and plans, but when you're under pressure a sense of limitations, restrictions and authoritarian strictures can arise.

MOON IN AQUARIUS: a quirky, outgoing phase during which trying new activities and new approaches to life will appeal. When you're under pressure the moon in Aquarius may stimulate unreliability, unconventionality or changeability.

MOON IN PISCES: a dreamy, introverted or artistic time in which music, the arts and romance will thrive; it is also a good time for meditation. When you're under pressure a Pisces moon can bring excessive daydreaming, forgetfulness or vagueness.

NB: if you know your moon sign you may find that when the moon is in your sign, as listed in this diary, life is either easier or more challenging depending on the planetary aspects to your moon at the time of your birth. Keep a note of the general mood or occurrences when the moon is in your sign and you may find that a pattern emerges.

Interplanetary aspects

Astrologers study the movements of planets in relation to each other. The measurements, which are in degrees, minutes and seconds, focus on patterns and particular aspects, which are the angles between the planets, the sun and other celestial objects. This diary includes mention of these aspects between the sun and the planets, and the terminology used is explained below – from 'opposition' (when a planet is opposite another) to 'quincunx' (when a planet is at a 150-degree angle to another).

The angles the planets and the sun make to one another have meanings in astrology. For example, a 'trine' aspect (120-degree angle) can be considered beneficial for the progress of your plans, while a 'square' aspect (90-degree angle) can present as a challenge (depending on your own attitude to challenges and obstacles).

By choosing dates carefully for the fruition of your plans you will be moving forward with the benefit of the knowledge of the cosmic influences that can help your progress.

NB: when you read the planetary aspects in this diary such as 'Sun square Uranus', be aware that the aspect's influence may span to a day before and a day after the actual date it is entered in this diary, especially regarding outer planets (Neptune, Uranus and Pluto). However, the moon phases are relevant for each day.

Planetary aspects

CONJUNCTION: when a celestial object is at the same degree and generally in the same sign of the zodiac as another celestial object and therefore is aligned from our point of view on earth. This can intensify the dynamics between the celestial objects and earth.

OPPOSITION: when a planet is opposite another, at a 180-degree angle. This can intensify the interplanetary dynamics.

SEXTILE: a 60-degree angle. This can be a peaceful, harmonious influence or it can facilitate the flow of energy between planetary influences.

SEMI-SEXTILE: a 30-degree angle. This is a harmonious aspect or it facilitates the flow of energy between planetary influences.

SQUARE: a 90-degree angle. This can be a challenging aspect, but as some people get going when the going gets tough it can lead to a breakthrough.

TRINE: a 120-degree angle. This can be a peaceful, harmonious influence or it can facilitate the flow of energy between planetary influences.

QUINCUNX: a 150-degree angle. This can present a hurdle to be overcome.

Retrogrades

Planets can appear to go backwards from our point of view on earth. The best-known retrograde phases are those of Mercury and Venus, although all other planets also turn retrograde and these retrograde phases are mentioned in this diary.

Retrograde phases can be a good time to assimilate, consolidate and integrate recent developments, although traditionally retrograde phases are associated with delays, a slowdown or difficult process. For example, a Mercury retrograde phase is often associated with difficult communications or traffic snarls, yet it can be an excellent time to integrate events and consolidate, review and re-order your ideas. This diary lists the start and finish dates of Mercury retrograde phases, as well as the kinds of activities that may be influenced by this phenomenon.

A 'station' is when planets turn from one direction to the other from our point of view on earth.

2023 NORTHERN HEMISPHERE MOON PHASES

JANUARY

S	M	T	W	T	F	S
1	2	3	4	5	6	7
8	9	10	11	12	13	14
15	16	17	18	19	20	21
22	23	24	25	26	27	28
29	30	31				

FEBRUARY

S	M	T	W	T	F	S
			1	2	3	4
5	6	7	8	9	10	11
12	13	14	15	16	17	18
19	20	21	22	23	24	25
26	27	28				

MARCH

S	M	T	W	T	F	S
			1	2	3	4
5	6	7	8	9	10	11
12	13	14	15	16	17	18
19	20	21	22	23	24	25
26	27	28	29	30	31	

APRIL

S	M	T	W	T	F	S
30						1
2	3	4	5	6	7	8
9	10	11	12	13	14	15
16	17	18	19	20	21	22
23	24	25	26	27	28	29

MAY

S	M	T	W	T	F	S
	1	2	3	4	5	6
7	8	9	10	11	12	13
14	15	16	17	18	19	20
21	22	23	24	25	26	27
28	29	30	31			

JUNE

S	M	T	W	T	F	S
				1	2	3
4	5	6	7	8	9	10
11	12	13	14	15	16	17
18	19	20	21	22	23	24
25	26	27	28	29	30	

2023 NORTHERN HEMISPHERE MOON PHASES

JULY

S	M	T	W	T	F	S
30	31					1
2	3	4	5	6	7	8
9	10	11	12	13	14	15
16	17	18	19	20	21	22
23	24	25	26	27	28	29

AUGUST

S	M	T	W	T	F	S
		1	2	3	4	5
6	7	8	9	10	11	12
13	14	15	16	17	18	19
20	21	22	23	24	25	26
27	28	29	30	31		

SEPTEMBER

S	M	T	W	T	F	S
					1	2
3	4	5	6	7	8	9
10	11	12	13	14	15	16
17	18	19	20	21	22	23
24	25	26	27	28	29	30

OCTOBER

S	M	T	W	T	F	S
1	2	3	4	5	6	7
8	9	10	11	12	13	14
15	16	17	18	19	20	21
22	23	24	25	26	27	28
29	30	31				

NOVEMBER

S	M	T	W	T	F	S
			1	2	3	4
5	6	7	8	9	10	11
12	13	14	15	16	17	18
19	20	21	22	23	24	25
26	27	28	29	30		

DECEMBER

S	M	T	W	T	F	S
31					1	2
3	4	5	6	7	8	9
10	11	12	13	14	15	16
17	18	19	20	21	22	23
24	25	26	27	28	29	30

○ New moon ● Full moon

January 2023

The sun entered Capricorn, 21 December 2022

New Year's Day begins with an intense conjunction between Venus and Pluto, ringing in the tone for 2023. If you are an intense, deep, thoughtful, passionate character you will love this phase, but if you prefer to keep things light-hearted this may be a tough beginning for the year, as it will bring out deeper feelings and impressions you sometimes prefer to circumnavigate.

Luckily, the Cancer full moon on 6 January will help you and everyone else gain a sense of perspective by bringing the importance of self-nurturance and nurturance of others into the frame.

Jupiter in Aries will add a sense of urgency and motivation to get things done this year, and to innovate and bring something new and exciting into your life. Jupiter will remain in proactive Aries until mid-May. Jupiter in Aries will encourage you to approach the year from a can-do point of view, producing both an optimistic outlook and one that takes into account the importance of taking action to attain your goals. In other words, if you want things to improve in your life you must do something about it.

Mercury will be retrograde until 18 January, making the first few weeks of the year ideal for reviewing where you are at now and what you can do differently. Aim to build a strong platform for yourself so that you are in a solid position to make the changes you wish to make during the year.

For Capricorns

The year begins with a retrograde Mercury in your sign, suggesting a melancholic, nostalgic atmosphere for you with the opportunity to reunite in person or at least to catch up with someone close by phone or online.

January is a good time to rethink or even rearrange your living situation and to plan ahead so that you're ready to make important changes in your personal and work circumstances according to your plans and financial prognosis for the year.

The sun trine Uranus aspect on 5 January points to a surprise meeting or news that will bring change to your home or personal life. Be prepared to innovate – don't forget, 'Be open minded, humanitarian and innovative' is the motto for the year!

The Cancer full moon on 6 January spells a fresh chapter in your personal life if you were born on or before that date, and at work and in your daily or health schedule if you were born later. Be prepared to factor your well-being into your plans for the next 12 months, as this will build a strong platform for you.

The Venus–Mars trine on 8–9 January will be ideal for romance and fun, just perfect for scheduling get-togethers over the weekend. Keep an eye on news around the 11th, 15th and 18th as developments during that week will inform you about the best way to move forward for the immediate future.

INTENTIONS *for the* YEAR

MONDAY 26 DECEMBER 2022)

TUESDAY 27)

WEDNESDAY 28)

THURSDAY 29)

FRIDAY 30 ◗

SATURDAY 31 ●

SUNDAY 1 ●

Venus conjunct Pluto: an intense start to the new year, and a good time to reconnect with those you love. Moon in Taurus.

JANUARY						
S	M	T	W	T	F	S
1	2	3	4	5	6	7
8	9	10	11	12	13	14
15	16	17	18	19	20	21
22	23	24	25	26	27	28
29	30	31				

MONDAY 2 ●

Mercury sextile Neptune; sun square Chiron: a lovely day for a trip somewhere beautiful and for reunions. However, this is also a time of stress, especially regarding health and well-being, so take things easy if you are under pressure. Moon in Taurus.

TUESDAY 3 ●

Venus enters Aquarius: a good day to try something new and to make connections with experts and those you love. Moon in Gemini.

WEDNESDAY 4 ●

Venus sextile Jupiter: a fresh start is possible, and there's no time like the present! Moon in Gemini.

THURSDAY 5 ●

Sun trine Uranus: expect unforeseen news and be adaptable to other people's ideas. Moon enters Cancer.

FRIDAY 6 ●

Full moon in Cancer: this full moon brings you together with those you love plus opens new opportunities for realistic and down-to-earth projects to take flight.

SATURDAY 7 ●

Sun conjunct Mercury: you will have the chance to review your paperwork. A reunion or news from the past will be important. It's a good day for health appointments. Moon in Cancer.

SUNDAY 8 ●

Mercury trine Uranus: expect unforeseen news. It's a good day for a trip and for meetings, but be prepared for something different. Moon in Leo.

JANUARY

S	M	T	W	T	F	S
1	2	3	4	5	6	7
8	9	10	11	12	13	14
15	16	17	18	19	20	21
22	23	24	25	26	27	28
29	30	31				

MONDAY 9   ●

Venus trine Mars: romance could flourish. It's a good day for get-togethers. Moon in Leo.

TUESDAY 10   ●

Moon enters Virgo.

WEDNESDAY 11   ●

Mercury square Chiron; Venus square moon's nodes: be prepared to consider someone else's point of view, even if news is not what you want to hear. Avoid arguments and look for fresh ways forward. You will get the chance to make new agreements. Avoid travel delays and misunderstandings. Moon in Virgo.

THURSDAY 12   ●

Mars ends its retrograde phase: a good time to consider new projects and the merits of leaving your comfort zone. Moon in Virgo.

FRIDAY 13

Sun sextile Neptune: Friday the 13th: lucky for some! Romance could flourish, so why not organise a date? You may enjoy a reunion. Moon in Libra.

SATURDAY 14

Sun semi-sextile Saturn: this is a good day for getting chores done and making a commitment to a plan or person. Moon in Libra.

SUNDAY 15

Venus square Uranus: you may need to reorganise an important plan or activity at short notice. Someone may be a little unpredictable. Be practical. Moon enters Scorpio.

JANUARY

S	M	T	W	T	F	S
1	2	3	4	5	6	7
8	9	10	11	12	13	14
15	16	17	18	19	20	21
22	23	24	25	26	27	28
29	30	31				

MONDAY 16   ☾

Moon in Scorpio.

TUESDAY 17   ☾

Mercury quincunx Mars: it's a good day for a health appointment. Avoid traffic delays and misunderstandings by planning ahead. Moon enters Sagittarius.

WEDNESDAY 18   ☾

Mercury ends its retrograde phase; sun conjunct Pluto: you may receive intense news or feel more emotional than usual, and for many this will be to do with work or health. Take time out when you can. Moon in Sagittarius.

THURSDAY 19   ☾

Moon enters Capricorn.

FRIDAY 20

The sun enters Aquarius: you may feel more adventurous and readier to develop your projects. Moon in Capricorn.

SATURDAY 21

New moon supermoon in Aquarius; Mercury quincunx Mars; Venus semi-sextile Neptune: a good time to do something new, but you must avoid making rash decisions as some communications may be confusing. Romance could blossom this weekend, so organise a treat. A good day for the arts, film, relaxation and a beauty treat.

SUNDAY 22

Uranus ends its retrograde phase; Venus conjunct Saturn: a good day for meetings and talks and for making commitments. You may consider a fresh financial strategy. An unpredictable person may behave true to character. Moon in Aquarius.

JANUARY

S	M	T	W	T	F	S
1	2	3	4	5	6	7
8	9	10	11	12	13	14
15	16	17	18	19	20	21
22	23	24	25	26	27	28
29	30	31				

January to
February 2023

Sun enters Aquarius, 20 January

The Aquarian new moon and supermoon on 21 January will kick-start an exciting chapter that will ask you to be more outgoing and innovative. If you like being proactive you'll enjoy this month, but if you generally prefer to avoid pushing yourself forward in life you may find this zodiacal month stressful. Ensure you have some stress-busting skill sets and techniques on hand such as regular exercise, meditation, gardening or creative endeavours.

You may experience intense developments around the new moon on 21 January and, if so, these will give you the heads-up about the kinds of new directions that will appeal.

The full moon in Leo on 5 February will shine a light on your projects and wishes. Consider how you wish to progress in the bigger picture in your life, as this full moon will ask you to bring your inner hero out to construct brave new foundations.

The square aspect between the full moon and innovative Uranus will ask you to look at constructive yet imaginative ways to forge a more adventurous but also caring path ahead, both for yourself and those you love.

News between 10 and 15 February will provide a heads-up as to how best to forge your path ahead in the most practical ways. It may involve returning to a previous circumstance or at the very least reviewing your options in realistic terms.

For Aquarians

It's all change for you over the next few weeks. Prepare to begin a fresh chapter in your personal life and at work. The new moon supermoon on 21 January will be ideal to kick-start a fresh daily routine that brings revitalising new practices into being on a daily basis. Be prepared to push yourself health-wise into new territory that enables you to re-imagine your own strengths and abilities.

The full moon on 5 February will help you to turn a corner in your personal life if you were born on or before that date and in your work and health-wise if you were born later. The concurrent Venus square Mars aspect may highlight what you really want merely because there are apparent obstacles.

However, there may also be big-picture developments such as travel or financial considerations that mean you must review very carefully where you stand. A health and work circumstance may take a turn that means you need to remain considerate of the circumstances of others, not just your own. A decision will be made in mid-February that will bring clarity to your circumstances.

MONDAY 23 ☽

Moon enters Pisces.

TUESDAY 24 ☽

Moon in Pisces.

WEDNESDAY 25 ☽

Venus semi-sextile Pluto: a good day for get-togethers. Moon enters Aries.

THURSDAY 26 ☽

Moon in Aries.

FRIDAY 27 ◗

Mercury square Chiron; Venus enters Pisces: be careful with communications as you may misinterpret someone's words and vice versa. Health and/or work and travel news will arise. Immerse yourself in the arts to unwind. Moon enters Taurus.

SATURDAY 28 ◗

Moon in Taurus.

SUNDAY 29 ◗

Moon in Taurus.

			JANUARY			
S	M	T	W	T	F	S
1	2	3	4	5	6	7
8	9	10	11	12	13	14
15	16	17	18	19	20	21
22	23	24	25	26	27	28
29	30	31				

MONDAY 30

Sun trine Mars; Mercury trine Uranus: a good day to be proactive and get in touch with people who could be helpful. Just avoid misunderstandings and be prepared to alter your schedule. Moon in Gemini.

TUESDAY 31

Venus semi-sextile Jupiter: a good day for get-togethers and financial decision-making and for personal development. Moon in Gemini.

WEDNESDAY 1

Sun sextile Chiron: this is a good day for improving health and well-being, both your own and someone else's, and for a fresh understanding of your own self-development. Moon enters Cancer.

THURSDAY 2

Moon in Cancer.

FRIDAY 3 ●

Moon in Cancer.

SATURDAY 4 ●

Sun square Uranus: you may find there is a spanner in the works, so be prepared to alter your plans at a moment's notice. Avoid taking unpredictable events personally. Moon enters Leo.

SUNDAY 5 ●

Full moon in Leo; Venus square Mars: the full moon will shine a light on what you really want deep down. If you are making long-range decisions, ensure these align with your big-picture values and spiritual beliefs. Avoid arguments as they could become long term.

FEBRUARY

S	M	T	W	T	F	S
			1	2	3	4
5	6	7	8	9	10	11
12	13	14	15	16	17	18
19	20	21	22	23	24	25
26	27	28				

MONDAY 6 ●

Mercury sextile Neptune: this is a lovely day to get together with like-minded people. You'll enjoy the arts, music and romance. Just avoid forgetfulness. Moon enters Virgo.

TUESDAY 7 ●

Moon in Virgo.

WEDNESDAY 8 ●

Venus sextile Uranus: a good day for get-togethers and being a little spontaneous. Moon in Virgo.

THURSDAY 9 ●

Mercury semi-sextile Saturn: a good day for talks and for making financial decisions. You may make a valid commitment now. Moon enters Libra.

FRIDAY 10

Mercury conjunct Pluto: talks are likely to be intense, and a trip may bring out strong feelings. Avoid impulsive decisions. Moon in Libra.

SATURDAY 11

Moon enters Scorpio.

SUNDAY 12

Sun semi-sextile Neptune: you'll enjoy getting together with like-minded, inspired people. It's a good day for creativity, the arts and romance. Romance could blossom. Moon in Scorpio.

FEBRUARY

S	M	T	W	T	F	S
			1	2	3	4
5	6	7	8	9	10	11
12	13	14	15	16	17	18
19	20	21	22	23	24	25
26	27	28				

MONDAY 13 ☾

Moon in Scorpio.

TUESDAY 14 ☾

Happy St Valentine's Day! Be adventurous, as it's a day for romance. Moon in Sagittarius.

WEDNESDAY 15 ☾

Venus conjunct Neptune: an ideal day for romance. You'll also enjoy the arts, and creative projects are likely to go well. Just avoid absent-mindedness. A good day to make financial decisions but you must ensure you have the facts. Moon in Sagittarius.

THURSDAY 16 ☾

Sun conjunct Saturn; Mercury square moon's north nodes: news will arrive that signals the need to be flexible about your projects and relationships. Avoid a battle of egos, as you could make a valuable commitment as a result. Moon in Capricorn.

FRIDAY 17 ☽

Moon in Capricorn.

SATURDAY 18 ☽

Sun enters Pisces; Mercury sextile Jupiter; Venus semi-sextile Saturn; Mars semi-sextile Uranus: be prepared to think outside the square. It's a good day for talks and meetings. An inspiring time awaits but you must be careful to follow your passions and interests and avoid being distracted. Moon in Aquarius.

SUNDAY 19 ☽

Venus sextile Pluto: a good day to deepen your relationship with someone special. You could make valuable changes you've been meaning to implement for a while. Moon in Aquarius.

FEBRUARY

S	M	T	W	T	F	S
			1	2	3	4
5	6	7	8	9	10	11
12	13	14	15	16	17	18
19	20	21	22	23	24	25
26	27	28				

february to
march 2023

Sun enters Pisces, 18 February

There will be no planets retrograde this zodiacal month, suggesting you can make great headway. The Pisces new moon and supermoon on 20 February is an ideal time to consider where your true priorities lie and how you wish to move forward in life. An old friend, teacher or acquaintance may be particularly influential or supportive at this time and could help you make important decisions.

The transit of Venus through Aries for the next three and a half weeks will bring a proactive feel to the month, providing a spring-fever vibe: it is time to make plans to improve your health, well-being and appearance and to enjoy better fitness and mental well-being.

However, the Virgo full moon on 7 March will spotlight the importance of being practical about your plans and avoiding charging ahead without due research. The conjunction just days prior of Jupiter, Venus and Chiron could even point out where you have made mistakes, so ensure you check facts if you are launching anything new from February to March. If you do the Venus-Jupiter-Chiron conjunction in early March is likely to have a cathartic and even potentially healing effect, especially for cardinal signs Aries, Cancer, Libra and Capricorn.

Tough aspects in mid-March are worth handling carefully to avoid arguments. When you do, these planetary alignments could be the motivation you need to make long-overdue changes in your life.

For Pisces

This Pisces season will provide you with the opportunity to get back on track in areas in which you feel you have lacked direction. The season kicks off with a bang, with the new moon supermoon in your sign on 20 February signalling the chance to get up to date with your various projects and ventures, especially if it's your birthday then. You're likely to be in touch with someone influential and helpful. If you need the help of an expert or mentor, they will be available then.

The transit of Mercury through your sign from 2 March will help boost your communications. The transit of Venus in Aries will provide a much-needed boost in energy and potentially even financially. If you have been unwell this will be a good time to boost your health and well-being. Enlist the help of an expert if necessary.

At the same time Saturn will enter your sign, bringing the chance to build stability and security over the next three years. However, it may also make you feel as though life is restrictive and limited and, if so, Saturn entering your sign will enable you to find new ways ahead.

The full moon in Virgo on 7 March will show whether your expectations have been unrealistic. There will be nothing amiss with delaying some plans if you discover they are simply not practical. Rely on innovation to devise something new that works on all levels.

The conjunction of Jupiter and Chiron on 12 March will point out how far you've come, but if you experience a hiccup see it as a hurdle that can be overcome. You'll gain a sense of progress in mid-March but you must be careful to avoid conflict in the process.

MONDAY 20 ○

New moon supermoon in Pisces; Mercury sextile Chiron; Venus enters Aries: a good time to consider your dreams and implement your intention to involve more art, romance and creativity in your life and to be proactive about gaining the life you want. This could be a healing time.

TUESDAY 21 ☽

Mercury square Uranus: be prepared to go the extra mile to ensure everyone is on the same page as you or you may experience travel delays and misunderstandings. Look outside the box at new ideas. Be inspired. Moon in Pisces.

WEDNESDAY 22 ☽

Mercury trine Mars: a better day than yesterday for talks and get-togethers. You may even have a light-bulb moment or will receive good news. Moon in Aries.

THURSADAY 23 ☽

Moon in Aries.

FRIDAY 24 ❯

*Sun sextile moon's north node: a lovely day for romance, so make a date!
You may bump into someone. A key meeting at work could take you closer
to a goal. Moon in Taurus.*

SATURDAY 25 ❯

Moon in Taurus.

SUNDAY 26 ❯

Moon enters Gemini.

FEBRUARY

S	M	T	W	T	F	S
			1	2	3	4
5	6	7	8	9	10	11
12	13	14	15	16	17	18
19	20	21	22	23	24	25
26	27	28				

MONDAY 27 ◗

Mercury semi-sextile Neptune: a good day for meetings and talks and also for shopping. Just avoid overindulging, as you may regret it. Moon in Gemini.

TUESDAY 28 ◗

Moon in Gemini.

WEDNESDAY 1 ◗

Moon in Cancer.

THURSDAY 2 ◗

Mercury enters Pisces; Venus conjunct Jupiter: a good time to focus on improving finances and self-esteem. A personal matter could blossom. Moon in Cancer.

FRIDAY 3 ●

Sun semi-sextile Jupiter; Venus conjunct Chiron: a good day for improving health and well-being and to make plans for work expansion or travel. This is likely to be a healing day. If you need expert help, reach out. If you are an expert you're likely to be busy. Moon enters Leo.

SATURDAY 4 ●

Moon in Leo.

SUNDAY 5 ●

Venus semi-sextile Uranus: expect a surprise. You'll enjoy being spontaneous. Moon in Leo.

MARCH

S	M	T	W	T	F	S
			1	2	3	4
5	6	7	8	9	10	11
12	13	14	15	16	17	18
19	20	21	22	23	24	25
26	27	28	29	30	31	

MONDAY 6 ●

Sun sextile Uranus: you'll enjoy an out-of-the-ordinary event and may be surprised by developments. Moon in Virgo.

TUESDAY 7 ●

Full moon in Virgo; Saturn enters Pisces: be prepared to think about the details of your various projects and plan ahead. Be practical about your ideas to avoid disappointment further down the line.

WEDNESDAY 8 ●

Moon enters Libra.

THURSDAY 9 ●

Moon in Libra.

FRIDAY 10 ●

Mercury semi-sextile Jupiter: a good day for meetings and to broach sensitive topics. If you're looking for work this is a good time to circulate your résumé and for interviews. Be optimistic but also practical. Moon in Libra.

SATURDAY 11 ●

Mercury sextile Uranus; Venus sextile Mars: be proactive and see your plans through to a good outcome. You may be surprised by beneficial news, but you must ensure you have the facts straight or mistakes can be made. Moon in Scorpio.

SUNDAY 12 ●

Jupiter conjunct Chiron: this is a good day to look after yourself and those you love. You'll enjoy the arts and music. Avoid gambling and minor accidents by being careful with your movements. Moon in Scorpio.

MARCH

S	M	T	W	T	F	S
			1	2	3	4
5	6	7	8	9	10	11
12	13	14	15	16	17	18
19	20	21	22	23	24	25
26	27	28	29	30	31	

MONDAY 13

Moon in Sagittarius.

TUESDAY 14

Mars square Neptune: have an open mind about people's opinions, but avoid being overly influenced as you may be easily misled. Be creative but avoid daydreaming, especially at work! Moon in Sagittarius.

WEDNESDAY 15

Sun conjunct Neptune: an ideal day for romance, the arts and love, but you may discover a mistake if you have not been vigilant with facts and figures. Moon enters Capricorn.

THURSDAY 16

Venus enters Taurus; sun square Mars; Mercury conjunct Neptune; Venus square Pluto: this may be an intense or busy day. Avoid a battle of egos. It's a lovely phase for looking after yourself and for treating yourself and others to a little luxury. Just avoid overindulging for the next few weeks! Moon in Capricorn.

FRIDAY 17   (

Sun conjunct Mercury; Mercury square Mars; Venus sextile Saturn:
conversations and developments may be fast moving, so ensure you're happy
with the way things are heading. If not, aim to slow things down if possible.
Moon enters Aquarius.

SATURDAY 18   (

Moon in Aquarius.

SUNDAY 19   (

Mercury enters Aries; Mercury sextile Pluto: a good day for talks, trips and
research. You may feel more energetic than usual, so organise an event!
Moon enters Pisces.

MARCH

S	M	T	W	T	F	S
			1	2	3	4
5	6	7	8	9	10	11
12	13	14	15	16	17	18
19	20	21	22	23	24	25
26	27	28	29	30	31	

March to April 2023

Sun enters Aries, 20 March

As the sun enters Aries it marks the spring equinox, a time when your plans and projects can gain momentum as the seeds you have sown so far this year begin to sprout.

This is another zodiacal month with no planets retrograde, so it's all systems go. If you prefer life to be calmer it's important to take measures to slow things down to avoid feeling under pressure.

A reunion or the chance to put right something from your past is not to be missed. You'll enjoy moving on as a result.

The Aries new moon on 21 March will be followed by the total solar eclipse, which will again be in Aries, on 20 April. This will be a motivating time, for some in a pleasant way and for others as a result of frustration or a feeling of antagonism. The key during this four-week period is to embrace the opportunity to dream a little, and then to make those dreams happen through positive and direct action.

Good health will be necessary to move ahead, especially in March, and the best way to overcome irritation and antagonism is to channel frustrated energy into upbeat projects rather than stewing on what's not working in your life. Be proactive now.

The Mercury square Pluto aspect on 3 April is best navigated carefully to avoid putting someone's back up. Be prepared to negotiate, and to be tactful and adaptable. The sun-Chiron conjunction on 5 April is again best tackled with diplomacy to avoid putting in motion a cycle you come to regret.

For Aries

This is your time of year, Aries, to show just what you have! You'll have a great opportunity to re-invent yourself and your life if this is what you want. It's likely at the very least you'll feel motivated to turn a corner in a key area of your life. However, you must avoid the temptation to express yourself forcefully, impulsively or aggressively. Assertiveness on the other hand will get you where you want to be now.

The new moon in Aries on 21 March will be conjunct Mercury, suggesting important health or personal news. You may find this is a poignant time, especially if it's your birthday. If you find this period a challenge you risk allowing your worst traits such as anger and bossiness to emerge, so you must avoid being your own worst enemy over the next four weeks. Focus instead on building the life you want in inspired ways. Be prepared to collaborate and co-operate with groups, organisations and friends.

The total solar eclipse in your sign on 20 April adds further weight to this being a key month and even a key year for change. It's the start of a significant new cycle for you, so plan big!

MONDAY 20

Sun enters Aries; sun sextile Pluto; Venus conjunct moon's north node; Jupiter semi-sextile Uranus: the spring equinox, a period of growth and a good time to make changes. A reunion or news from the past may be significant. You may hear from someone unexpectedly. Moon in Pisces.

TUESDAY 21

New moon in Aries: a good time to start something new, especially if it involves writing, speaking, publishing, communications in general or contracts.

WEDNESDAY 22

Moon in Aries.

THURSDAY 23

Pluto enters Aquarius: look out for a new way to approach people and long-term projects and goals. Moon enters Taurus.

FRIDAY 24　　　　　　　　　　　　　　　　　　　　　　)

Moon in Taurus.

SATURDAY 25　　　　　　　　　　　　　　　　　　　　　　)

*Mars enters Cancer; sun semi-sextile moon's north node; Mars quincunx
Pluto: an intuitive approach to someone will work if you feel conflicted about
a relationship. Look for new ways to express yourself. Avoid rash decisions.
Moon in Taurus.*

SUNDAY 26　　　　　　　　　　　　　　　　　　　　　　)

*Mercury conjunct Chiron: there are healing aspects to the day. It's a good time
to look after yourself and someone close. Moon in Gemini.*

MARCH

S	M	T	W	T	F	S
			1	2	3	4
5	6	7	8	9	10	11
12	13	14	15	16	17	18
19	20	21	22	23	24	25
26	27	28	29	30	31	

MONDAY 27

Mercury semi-sextile Uranus: you may receive surprise news. Be adaptable and open minded for the best results. Moon in Gemini.

TUESDAY 28

Mercury conjunct Jupiter: a good day for talks, financial decisions and travel. Just avoid exaggerated expectations. Moon enters Cancer.

WEDNESDAY 29

Moon in Cancer.

THURSDAY 30

Venus conjunct Uranus; Mars trine Saturn: you may experience a surprise, and you'll enjoy doing something different. It's a good day for making important decisions and commitments. Use your intuition for the best results. Moon enters Leo.

FRIDAY 31 ●

Moon in Leo.

SATURDAY 1 ●

Mercury semi-sextile Neptune: you'll enjoy a little romance. You may hear ideal news. It's a good day for a trip somewhere beautiful and to enjoy the arts and creativity. Moon in Leo.

SUNDAY 2 ●

Venus semi-sextile Jupiter: this is a good time to be practical about adventurous plans, otherwise you may be inclined to be idealistic. It's a good day for get-togethers and financial planning. Moon enters Virgo.

APRIL

S	M	T	W	T	F	S
						1
2	3	4	5	6	7	8
9	10	11	12	13	14	15
16	17	18	19	20	21	22
23	24	25	26	27	28	29
30						

MONDAY 3 ●

Mercury enters Taurus; Mercury square Pluto: be patient, adaptable and tactful, as delays and misunderstandings are likely. Plan ahead to avoid mishaps and back up computers for the best measure. Moon in Virgo.

TUESDAY 4 ●

Moon enters Libra.

WEDNESDAY 5 ●

Sun conjunct Chiron; Mercury sextile Saturn: it's a good day for a health appointment and meetings and to sort out financial matters. Moon in Libra.

THURSDAY 6 ●

Full moon in Libra; Mercury conjunct moon's north node: a good time to find more balance in your life through music, good health and adopting an optimistic attitude. You'll hear key news from or meet someone from your past.

FRIDAY 7 ●

Sun semi-sextile Uranus; Venus sextile Neptune: expect a surprise. It's a good day to be spontaneous. Romance could blossom. Avoid forgetfulness. Moon enters Scorpio.

SATURDAY 8 ●

Mercury sextile Mars: a good day to take the initiative with talks and meetings. Avoid pre-empting outcomes and impulsiveness. Moon in Scorpio.

SUNDAY 9 ●

Moon enters Sagittarius.

APRIL

S	M	T	W	T	F	S
						1
2	3	4	5	6	7	8
9	10	11	12	13	14	15
16	17	18	19	20	21	22
23	24	25	26	27	28	29
30						

MONDAY 10

Moon in Sagittarius.

TUESDAY 11

Venus enters Gemini; sun conjunct Jupiter; Venus trine Pluto: a meeting or news will be significant. Communications are likely to get busier or more varied and upbeat. A financial matter is best dealt with carefully and with a long-term view. Romance and socialising could be fulfilling. Moon enters Capricorn.

WEDNESDAY 12

Moon in Capricorn.

THURSDAY 13

Moon enters Aquarius.

FRIDAY 14 ☽

Venus square Saturn; Saturn sextile moon's north node: it's a good day to discuss and sort out financial matters, with an expert if necessary. You may meet someone you feel a strong link with. Matters you disagree over are best approached from a long-term point of view. Moon in Aquarius.

SATURDAY 15 ☽

Moon enters Pisces.

SUNDAY 16 ☽

Sun semi-sextile Neptune: a good day to relax and find time for the arts, film, music and romance. Avoid forgetfulness and overindulgence as you'll regret it! Moon in Pisces.

APRIL

S	M	T	W	T	F	S
						1
2	3	4	5	6	7	8
9	10	11	12	13	14	15
16	17	18	19	20	21	22
23	24	25	26	27	28	29
30						

MONDAY 17   (

Moon in Pisces.

TUESDAY 18   (

Moon in Aries.

WEDNESDAY 19   (

Moon in Aries.

THURSDAY 20   ○

Sun enters Taurus; total solar eclipse in Aries; sun square Pluto: be prepared for change, and avoid stubbornness and resistance but also impulsiveness. It's a good time to be practical and realistic. Moon enters Taurus.

FRIDAY 21)

Mercury turns retrograde: keep an eye on communications as key information may come your way. It's a good time over the coming weeks to review and revise your circumstances. Moon in Taurus.

SATURDAY 22)

Moon enters Gemini.

SUNDAY 23)

Moon in Gemini.

APRIL

S	M	T	W	T	F	S
						1
2	3	4	5	6	7	8
9	10	11	12	13	14	15
16	17	18	19	20	21	22
23	24	25	26	27	28	29
30						

April to May 2023

Sun enters Taurus, 20 April

This is one of two eclipse seasons this year. The next four weeks provide the chance to incubate something new. It's an excellent time to be practical and hands-on with your plans and ideas, as the Aries total solar eclipse on 20 April will enable you to move ahead in dynamic ways and to kick-start exciting plans.

This is therefore the time to innovate new ideas and plans, and also coincidentally to embrace your intuitive side. Mars in Cancer will encourage you to express your instinctive abilities in fresh ways. Just watch out for being super sensitive: this phase may lead you to take things personally.

It's imperative to be adaptable and flexible, or the heavily Taurean signature of this zodiacal month will create a stubborn, stick-in-the-mud attitude that will be frustrating. The solar eclipse on 20 April will be in Aries, square Pluto, suggesting those who do not adapt well to change may find this phase difficult.

The solar eclipse will be the main factor driving things forward, so it really is a date to put in the calendar to be prepared for change. Although it falls on the same day as the sun enters Taurus this eclipse will be in the last degree of Aries, adding a sense of urgency that change is necessary and especially for Aries and the cardinal and fixed signs.

Mercury turns retrograde the next day for three weeks and communications will not be back at their best until early June, so it's vital to communicate clearly.

These four weeks will be ideal for reviewing paperwork, ideas and even relationship decisions if necessary, so this needn't be a time of difficulty or strife if you use it for reflection and re-organisation, especially if you feel you have gone off the path. Luckily, Jupiter's entry into practical and grounded Taurus on 16 May will provide a sense of cautious optimism and the ability to take things in your stride.

For Taureans

The total solar eclipse on 20 April suggests that the past must be left behind and the present is to be revealed. This is a marvellous opportunity to move your life forward in the right direction, but you must avoid knee-jerk reactions to events that seem to block your path. Focus on opening a gate to new options. If you were born at the end of April or in early May you will be especially drawn to initiate bold change, and there may be challenges as you must embrace fresh ideas and even beliefs and find new ways to relate with people.

The penumbral lunar eclipse in Scorpio on 5 May will be an intense full moon, especially if it's your birthday. The sun's conjunction with unpredictable Uranus on 9 May will enable you to look outside the box at your options, especially in your personal life. Be prepared to diversify at work.

The Taurus new moon on 19 May will present another key opportunity to turn a corner, especially if it's your birthday. Jupiter enters your sign on 16 May, kick-starting an abundant phase that will take you through well into 2024; this is enough reason to adopt a positive mindset.

MONDAY 24)

Mercury semi-sextile Venus; Mercury sextile Mars; Venus semi-sextile Mars: a good time to get in touch with an old friend or clear up past paperwork and financial matters. Moon enters Cancer.

TUESDAY 25)

Sun sextile Saturn: a good day for meetings and making agreements, both in your personal life and financially. Moon in Cancer.

WEDNESDAY 26)

Moon in Cancer.

THURSDAY 27)

Venus semi-sextile Uranus: you'll enjoy doing something different and may hear unexpected news. Moon enters Leo.

FRIDAY 28

Moon in Leo.

SATURDAY 29

Mars sextile Uranus: a good day for taking the initiative, especially with new projects and ideas. You may feel spontaneous and ready to embrace a new plan. Just avoid making rash decisions. Moon enters Virgo.

SUNDAY 30

Moon in Virgo.

APRIL

S	M	T	W	T	F	S
						1
2	3	4	5	6	7	8
9	10	11	12	13	14	15
16	17	18	19	20	21	22
23	24	25	26	27	28	29
30						

MONDAY 1 ●

Pluto turns retrograde: you may find you have a little more time to review some of your plans over the coming weeks. Moon in Virgo.

TUESDAY 2 ●

Sun conjunct Mercury; Jupiter semi-sextile Neptune: news will help you understand something from the past. You may enjoy a reunion. The arts, music and romance will appeal. If you are making decisions, avoid being idealistic; get the facts instead. Moon in Libra.

WEDNESDAY 3 ●

Moon in Libra.

THURSDAY 4 ●

Venus square Neptune: be prepared to research details and avoid distractions. You may be absent-minded and idealistic, so keep your feet on the ground. Avoid giving mixed messages. Moon enters Scorpio.

FRIDAY 5 ●

Lunar eclipse in Scorpio; Venus sextile Jupiter: emotions are likely to be strong and you may be surprised by some people's reactions to events. Maintain a grounded approach. You could make progress both in financial and personal contexts.

SATURDAY 6 ●

Moon enters Sagittarius.

SUNDAY 7 ●

Venus enters Cancer; Venus quincunx Pluto: increased focus on self-nurture and nurturance of others will appeal both today and over the coming month. Be prepared to understand someone else's values, even if you disagree. Moon in Sagittarius.

MAY

S	M	T	W	T	F	S
	1	2	3	4	5	6
7	8	9	10	11	12	13
14	15	16	17	18	19	20
21	22	23	24	25	26	27
28	29	30	31			

MONDAY 8   ●

Moon in Sagittarius.

TUESDAY 9   ●

Sun conjunct Uranus: you're likely to experience a surprise. You or someone close may be feeling a little unpredictable. Moon in Capricorn.

WEDNESDAY 10   ◐

Moon in Capricorn.

THURSDAY 11   ◑

Moon in Aquarius.

FRIDAY 12 ◐

Mercury sextile Saturn: a good day to review some of your decisions, especially those to do with finances, health and work. You may hear from an old friend. Moon in Aquarius.

SATURDAY 13 ◐

Mercury sextile Venus; Venus trine Saturn: you are likely to receive good news and will enjoy a get-together. It's a good day to review finances. If you're shopping you may find a good buy, but must avoid overspending. Moon in Pisces.

SUNDAY 14 ◐

Moon in Pisces.

MAY

S	M	T	W	T	F	S
	1	2	3	4	5	6
7	8	9	10	11	12	13
14	15	16	17	18	19	20
21	22	23	24	25	26	27
28	29	30	31			

MONDAY 15 ◖

Mercury ends its retrograde phase; Mars trine Neptune: prepare for key news, especially if it's your birthday at the end of April. Be prepared to move ahead with agreements and communications. You'll enjoy the arts and romance. A trip somewhere beautiful will appeal. Moon enters Aries.

TUESDAY 16 ◖

Jupiter enters Taurus: a new 12-month phase begins, a good phase in which to be focused, practical and mindful of the importance of the earth and your environment. Moon in Aries.

WEDNESDAY 17 ◖

Moon enters Taurus.

THURSDAY 18 ◖

Jupiter square Pluto: you can accomplish a great deal, and the key lies in being ready to talk and adapt. This could be an intense day, so be prepared to take things one step at a time. Moon in Taurus.

FRIDAY 19 ○

New moon in Taurus; Mercury sextile Saturn: a good time to be realistic and put carefully laid plans in motion. Financial agreements could be made. Moon enters Gemini.

SATURDAY 20 ☽

Mars enters Leo: this signals a more energetic five weeks ahead but could also point to a rise in conflict and arguments, so be tactful when possible. Moon in Gemini.

SUNDAY 21 ☽

Sun enters Gemini; sun trine Pluto; Mars opposite Pluto: be prepared for news and developments that will signal change and the chance to move forward. Be flexible and avoid conflict as it will escalate quickly. Moon in Gemini.

MAY

S	M	T	W	T	F	S
	1	2	3	4	5	6
7	8	9	10	11	12	13
14	15	16	17	18	19	20
21	22	23	24	25	26	27
28	29	30	31			

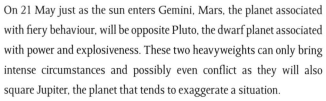

May to June 2023

Sun enters Gemini, 21 May

On 21 May just as the sun enters Gemini, Mars, the planet associated with fiery behaviour, will be opposite Pluto, the dwarf planet associated with power and explosiveness. These two heavyweights can only bring intense circumstances and possibly even conflict as they will also square Jupiter, the planet that tends to exaggerate a situation.

The fixed signs involved in this astrological formation point to stubbornness, pride and potential conflict – that is, unless you can find room for negotiation, in which case there can be much progress in many areas of your life. However, you must be prepared to adapt to the new. The next 10 days will benefit from a considerate and moderate approach, as pressure will be on and tempers likely to flare. If you need to get things done this phase is ideal for focusing on your goals.

During June it's important to keep your communication skills in top condition, especially if you find that some relationships and communications stall. Luckily, the sun and Mercury in Gemini will help with this endeavour.

Travel and decisions related to trips and those you love who are far away will merit careful thought. Retrograde Pluto's re-entry into Capricorn on 11 June may slow some plans down, but if you can take advantage of this time to perfect your plans you will make solid progress. The Gemini new moon on 18 June is a good time to make a wish for more flexibility in your movements and provides the chance to boost communications and travel options.

For Geminis

This will be a good month to move forward with fresh plans and ideas, even if it seems at times that the odds are against you. And while you prefer life to be light-hearted, you may for this reason find the upcoming four weeks challenging. If you have already found ways to manage difficulties and pressures in life you will excel this month, and your particular abilities – namely good communication and networking skills – will be useful now.

The full moon in Sagittarius on 4 June signals the start of an adventurous cycle for you, especially in your business or personal relationships if you were born before 4 June and at work or health-wise if you were born after 4 June.

The entry of Mercury in your sign on 11 June and its trine with Pluto suggests you will manage to pick up a project or relationship where you left off. As well, the new moon in your sign on 18 June will further corroborate the idea that you are beginning something entirely new, which is very exciting indeed.

MONDAY 22 〉

Sun semi-sextile Jupiter; sun sextile Mars: a good day to get things done, so be proactive. Be optimistic but also realistic to avoid exaggerated expectations. Moon enters Cancer.

TUESDAY 23 〉

Mars square Jupiter: you could get a lot done but you must avoid conflict if obstacles arise, as it could flare up. Moon in Cancer.

WEDNESDAY 24 〉

Moon enters Leo.

THURSDAY 25 〉

Moon in Leo.

FRIDAY 26

Venus sextile Uranus: someone or something may surprise you. You'll enjoy being spontaneous and outgoing. Moon in Leo.

SATURDAY 27

Moon enters Virgo.

SUNDAY 28

Sun square Saturn: a good day to focus on what's important, including housework, duties and responsibilities and those you love, and then you can relax! If you think ahead, a delay or obstacles needn't derail your plans. Moon in Virgo.

MAY

S	M	T	W	T	F	S
	1	2	3	4	5	6
7	8	9	10	11	12	13
14	15	16	17	18	19	20
21	22	23	24	25	26	27
28	29	30	31			

MONDAY 29   ●

Moon enters Libra.

TUESDAY 30   ●

Moon in Libra.

WEDNESDAY 31   ●

Moon in Libra.

THURSDAY 1   ●

Mars quincunx Saturn: a good time to double-check your plans and the details of work and financial matters to avoid mistakes. You could make great progress with ventures but you must pace yourself. Moon in Scorpio.

FRIDAY 2 ●

*Jupiter conjunct moon's north node: a reunion or catch-up will be significant.
Moon in Scorpio.*

SATURDAY 3 ●

Moon enters Sagittarius.

SUNDAY 4 ●

*Full moon in Sagittarius; Mercury conjunct Uranus: expect unforeseen news.
You may bump into an old friend or experience something unusual. There is a
healing element to do with this full moon. Take a moment to consider how you
can boost your health and well-being and that of others in the long term and
make plans.*

JUNE

S	M	T	W	T	F	S
				1	2	3
4	5	6	7	8	9	10
11	12	13	14	15	16	17
18	19	20	21	22	23	24
25	26	27	28	29	30	

MONDAY 5 ●

Venus enters Leo; Venus opposite Pluto: this may be an intense day with thoughts and feelings that are hard to ignore. Be patient but prepared to voice your opinions and values in a measured way. Avoid conflict; it is likely to escalate. Moon enters Capricorn.

TUESDAY 6 ●

Moon in Capricorn.

WEDNESDAY 7 ●

Moon enters Aquarius.

THURSDAY 8 ●

Moon in Aquarius.

FRIDAY 9

Mercury sextile Neptune: a lovely day to talk and indulge in the arts, romance and music. Just avoid misunderstandings and forgetfulness. Moon enters Pisces.

SATURDAY 10

Moon in Pisces.

SUNDAY 11

Mercury enters Gemini; Pluto enters Capricorn; Mercury trine Pluto: this is a good time to re-evaluate some of your plans and projects. You may enjoy a reunion or plan a return to an old haunt. Moon enters Aries.

JUNE

S	M	T	W	T	F	S
				1	2	3
4	5	6	7	8	9	10
11	12	13	14	15	16	17
18	19	20	21	22	23	24
25	26	27	28	29	30	

MONDAY 12 ◖

Moon in Aries.

TUESDAY 13 ◖

Venus quincunx Saturn: double-check that everyone is on the same page and avoid making assumptions, especially concerning money, principles and values. Moon enters Taurus.

WEDNESDAY 14 ◖

Moon in Taurus.

THURSDAY 15 ◖

Mercury semi-sextile Jupiter; Mercury square Saturn: a good day to negotiate, but developments may not all be smooth sailing. However, if you're cautious and choose your words carefully you could make great progress. Avoid delays and mix-ups. Moon in Taurus.

FRIDAY 16   (

Moon in Gemini.

SATURDAY 17   (

*Saturn turns retrograde; Mercury sextile Venus: you'll enjoy a get-together.
If you're shopping, ensure you can return your purchase if you decide you no
longer want it when you get home. Moon in Gemini.*

SUNDAY 18   ○

*New moon in Gemini: this is a positive new moon for making a wish, especially
to do with finances and any arrangement you want to stabilise. Just ensure you
have the correct facts first. Moon enters Cancer.*

JUNE

S	M	T	W	T	F	S
				1	2	3
4	5	6	7	8	9	10
11	12	13	14	15	16	17
18	19	20	21	22	23	24
25	26	27	28	29	30	

MONDAY 19)

Sun square Neptune; Jupiter sextile Saturn: a good day to make agreements, but if you feel slightly forgetful and nostalgic take a moment to centre yourself. It's a good day for the arts, but you must be patient with delays and obstacles. Moon in Cancer.

TUESAY 20)

Moon enters Leo.

WEDNESDAY 21)

Sun enters Cancer; sun quincunx Pluto: as the sun enters Cancer this is the summer solstice, a time to bask in high summer and the enjoyment of the harvest soon to come. Be prepared to see another's viewpoint but to tactfully stand up for your values if need be. Moon in Leo.

THURSDAY 22)

Moon in Leo.

FRIDAY 23

Sun sextile moon's north node; Mars trine Chiron: you'll enjoy a reunion or a return to an old haunt. It's a good day to deepen spirituality and relationships. You may be inclined to focus on well-being. Moon enters Virgo.

SATURDAY 24

Moon in Virgo.

SUNDAY 25

Mercury square Neptune: a lovely day to dream, but if you're working avoid forgetfulness and focus on details. Travel and communications may be delayed or confusing. Moon enters Libra.

JUNE						
S	M	T	W	T	F	S
				1	2	3
4	5	6	7	8	9	10
11	12	13	14	15	16	17
18	19	20	21	22	23	24
25	26	27	28	29	30	

June to July 2023

Sun enters Cancer, 21 June

When the sun enters Cancer it marks the summer solstice in the northern hemisphere. The day is the longest, and we begin to turn our minds to the harvest time arriving soon. It is a time when your activities may peak and you realise the importance of self-nurture and nurturance of others so that you attain your greatest collective potential.

At the same time this year Mars will trine Chiron, suggesting health, well-being and learning will be strong features of the upcoming month.

Expect significant news and developments at the end of June and around the full moon on 3 July. Developments will provide adequate clarity about the best step for you to take next. If you have been contemplating travel, news at this time will be decisive.

This may also be a time when you must make key financial decisions. Commitments made now are likely to be constructive at the very least – with one proviso: that you research your circumstances adequately and avoid impulsive actions you are likely to regret.

Developments around the Cancerian new moon on 17 July will further emphasise the need to consider your actions carefully to avoid mistakes. Find new ways to communicate if your relationships are strained. This new moon will be a good time to consider how to re-invent your life if you feel it is in dire need of an overhaul. You will undergo challenges, but rest assured that with a nurturing approach you can overcome obstacles.

For Cancerians

You're known for your nurturing abilities, both of yourself and others. And this year during your own zodiacal month your skill sets will be stronger than ever. It's possible you can make huge strides forwards, so if you've been feeling under the weather or someone close has been unwell this is prime time to find healthier ways forward.

The full moon on 3 July will be an especially auspicious time to make a health pledge to move forward in your life with a healthier outlook in all aspects: mentally, physically, emotionally and spiritually.

The new moon in your sign on 17 July further emphasises the need to find new ways to self-nurture and nurture others. In addition, with careful communications you could re-invent your circumstances even if there is pressure to maintain the status quo. Be creative and inspired and follow your hunches. This new moon will be trine Neptune, the planet associated with spiritual understanding, so trust you are supported by greater powers than your own. However, Neptune is also the planet associated with misguidance, so if you're making long-term decisions ensure you research facts adequately to avoid being misled.

MONDAY 26 ◗

Mars square Uranus: avoid traffic delays and making rash decisions by planning ahead. Moon in Libra.

TUESDAY 27 ◗

Mercury enters Cancer; Mercury sextile moon's north node: you'll enjoy getting together with like-minded people. You could make solid financial decisions with the right information. Trust your instincts over the coming weeks. Moon in Libra.

WEDNESDAY 28 ●

Moon enters Scorpio.

THURSDAY 29 ●

Sun trine Saturn; Venus trine Chiron: a good day to get things done, and for meetings and constructive talks. It's also a good day to make a commitment and for financial and health- and beauty-related decisions. Moon in Scorpio.

FRIDAY 30 ●

Sun conjunct Mercury; Mercury trine Saturn: a good day for get-togethers and to make financial agreements and commitments. Moon enters Sagittarius.

SATURDAY 1 ●

Sun and Mercury sextile Jupiter: expect news. A trip or meeting will be productive, and you may feel adventurous and outgoing. If you're shopping you may find something lovely, but you must avoid overspending. Moon in Sagittarius.

SUNDAY 2 ●

Venus square Uranus: expect a surprise. You may need to re-evaluate a decision or a plan. Moon enters Capricorn.

JULY

S	M	T	W	T	F	S
						1
2	3	4	5	6	7	8
9	10	11	12	13	14	15
16	17	18	19	20	21	22
23	24	25	26	27	28	29
30	31					

MONDAY 3 ●

Full moon in Capricorn: you may receive key news. Make arrangements that will provide a secure and stable way forward.

TUESDAY 4 ●

Moon enters Aquarius.

WEDNESDAY 5 ●

Moon in Aquarius.

THURSDAY 6 ●

Mercury square Chiron; Mars quincunx Neptune: avoid making rash financial and personal decisions. This is a good day for improving health and well-being, especially if you have felt under the weather. Someone may need your help or you may need someone's help, in which case an expert will be beneficial. Moon enters Pisces.

FRIDAY 7

Mercury sextile Uranus: you'll enjoy experiencing something new or a surprise get-together. Just check the details first to avoid delays. Moon in Pisces.

SATURDAY 8

Mercury semi-sextile Venus: a lovely day for get-togethers and to improve relationships, so take the initiative. It's a good day to sort out finances. If you are shopping avoid overspending, especially if you're already in debt. Moon enters Aries.

SUNDAY 9

Mars quincunx Pluto: a little tension in the air fosters romance, but if there's too much stress it can be a real passion killer. Aim to calm things down if necessary. Moon in Aries.

JULY

S	M	T	W	T	F	S
						1
2	3	4	5	6	7	8
9	10	11	12	13	14	15
16	17	18	19	20	21	22
23	24	25	26	27	28	29
30	31					

MONDAY 10   ☾

Mars enters Virgo; Mercury trine Neptune: a good day for creativity and artistic pursuits. Romantic words will not fall on deaf ears. Maintain focus at work. You may feel extravagant. Moon in Aries.

TUESDAY 11   ☾

Mercury enters Leo: communications may become more upbeat but also less guarded over the coming weeks. Avoid taking people's opinions personally. Moon in Taurus.

WEDNESDAY 12   ☾

Sun square Chiron: be prepared to be adaptable, but apply the brakes if you feel developments are heading in the wrong direction. You will benefit from looking at an ongoing personal or health matter in a new light. Moon in Taurus.

THURSDAY 13   ☾

Moon enters Gemini.

FRIDAY 14   (

Sun sextile Uranus; Mercury quincunx Saturn: it's a lovely day for socialising, and you may be drawn to experiencing something new. If you're shopping you may need to curb your spending. Avoid feeling Rome can be built in one day relationship-wise. Moon in Gemini.

SATURDAY 15   (

Moon enters Cancer.

SUNDAY 16   (

Venus quincunx Neptune: be clear about what you want in your life and from someone close. You may be inclined to overindulge, which you'll regret! Moon in Cancer.

JULY						
S	M	T	W	T	F	S
						1
2	3	4	5	6	7	8
9	10	11	12	13	14	15
16	17	18	19	20	21	22
23	24	25	26	27	28	29
30	31					

MONDAY 17 ○

New moon in Cancer; Mercury square Jupiter; moon's north node enters Aries: this new moon asks that you find fresh ways to self-nurture and nurture others, especially if developments are intense. Be careful with communications and avoid travel delays by planning ahead. Be prepared to start something new.

TUESDAY 18)

Moon in Leo.

WEDNESDAY 19)

Moon in Leo.

THURSDAY 20)

Sun trine Neptune: this is a lovely day to follow inspiration where it takes you. The arts, music and creativity will all flourish and so, too, will romance, so organise a date! Moon enters Virgo.

FRIDAY 21 ☽

Mars opposite Saturn: you or someone close will be keen to make arrangements and plans for the future. Avoid feeling pressured into something you're not ready for, but be prepared to commit to something if it resonates. Moon in Virgo.

SATUDAY 22 ☽

Sun opposite Pluto; sun square moon's nodes; Mercury trine Chiron: you may feel intensely about someone or an issue. Double-check your emotions aren't running away with you and be prepared to make a bold statement if it's relevant. You may enjoy a reunion or a return to an old haunt. If you need help it will be available. Moon in Virgo.

SUNDAY 23 ☽

Sun enters Leo; Mercury square Uranus; Venus turns retrograde: you may experience an unusual event. Avoid misunderstandings and mix-ups. Be prepared to consider someone's opinions. Avoid travel delays by planning ahead. Moon enters Libra.

JULY

S	M	T	W	T	F	S
						1
2	3	4	5	6	7	8
9	10	11	12	13	14	15
16	17	18	19	20	21	22
23	24	25	26	27	28	29
30	31					

July to August 2023

Sun enters Leo, 23 July

As the sun enters Leo it will be opposite retrograde Pluto and square the moon's nodes, and Venus will begin a retrograde phase. All up there is likely to be a degree of inner conflict about a situation or person. Be sure to act on your feelings and your loyalties to those you have strong soul connections with. Avoid making hasty decisions as Venus retrograde will allow you to monitor how you feel and make well-considered decisions over the coming weeks.

Some meetings and discussions at the end of July will thrill you while others may leave you cold, so the key then will be to discern who and what resonates most deeply and what or who is best left in your past.

The full moon supermoon in Aquarius on 1 August will ask that you look at life from a fresh perspective, especially in connection with your learning curve and activities you wish to expand. Be prepared to look at life from outside the square, and aim to be practical while also being imaginative and innovative.

The period from 9 to 10 August could be a little tense, so aim to improve communication skills during this time to avoid conflict. A healing opportunity on the weekend of 12 to 13 August is not to be missed. It will be a good time to look after your own health and to also nurture others.

The new moon in Leo on 16 August offers the chance to turn a corner and be adventurous and proactive, but with a word of caution: if you have not researched your circumstances adequately this could be a true disadvantage, so be wise. Consider your options carefully and engage the expertise of advisers and experts if necessary.

For Leos

The next few weeks could be transformative both at work and health-wise, especially if you were born at the end of July or in mid-August. All Leos will find the full moon supermoon on 1 August particularly potent, as it will offer the chance to turn a corner either in your personal life if you were born at the end of July or in your daily schedule at work and health-wise if you were born in August.

The Leo new moon on 16 August has a powerful healing quality about it, so it is an excellent time to venture forward with health and well-being initiatives and infuse your life with more optimism. Place your intention on turning a corner, and this could be a key turning point for you. Just be practical as well as adventurous.

The level of success you can expect now is determined by the level of attention to detail you place on your activities – without becoming obsessive! With a balanced approach all is possible now, even if you sometimes feel you're simply going over old ground. See this as the opportunity to iron out any creases in your existing plans.

MONDAY 24

Moon in Libra.

TUESDAY 25

Moon enters Scorpio.

WDNESDAY 26

Moon in Scorpio.

THURSDAY 27

Mercury conjunct Venus; Mercury quincunx Neptune: you may enjoy a reunion. Inspiration and imagination will certainly help move any issues forward, but you must be prepared to carefully evaluate your options. You may need to review circumstances and avoid impulsiveness. Moon in Scorpio.

FRIDAY 28 ●

Mercury enters Virgo; Mercury trine moon's north node; Mercury quincunx Pluto; Pluto square moon's nodes: you may reconsider your feelings. It's a good day for examining the details of developments and working towards an outcome, but you must avoid overanalysis and perfectionism. Moon in Sagittarius.

SATURDAY 29 ●

Sun quincunx Saturn: a good day for housework and gardening, and for getting finances shipshape. You may need to work a little harder at your usual chores, but when you do you will succeed. Moon in Sagittarius.

SUNDAY 30 ●

Venus quincunx Neptune: what you want right now is to relax, so go about making it happen – otherwise the day will run away with you! It's a good day for romance and the arts, but you must get organised first. Moon in Capricorn.

JULY						
S	M	T	W	T	F	S
						1
2	3	4	5	6	7	8
9	10	11	12	13	14	15
16	17	18	19	20	21	22
23	24	25	26	27	28	29
30	31					

MONDAY 31 ●

Moon in Capricorn.

TUESDAY 1 ●

Full moon and supermoon in Aquarius; Mars trine Jupiter: a good day to be proactive and aim for your goals in practical, realistic yet innovative ways, especially if there is an obstacle to overcome.

WEDNESDAY 2 ●

Mercury opposite Saturn: a good time to discuss financial matters and make solid agreements that could move your financial situation forward. You may not agree with everyone so you must take the most practical route forward. Moon in Aquarius.

THURSDAY 3 ●

Moon in Pisces.

FRIDAY 4 ●

Moon in Pisces.

SATURDAY 5 ●

Moon in Aries.

SUNDAY 6 ●

Moon in Aries.

AUGUST						
S	M	T	W	T	F	S
		1	2	3	4	5
6	7	8	10	10	11	12
13	14	15	16	17	18	19
20	21	22	23	24	25	26
27	28	29	30	31		

MONDAY 7

Sun square Jupiter: a good time to take on board other people's viewpoints while being careful to honour your own without causing conflict. Moon enters Taurus.

TUESDAY 8

Moon in Taurus.

WEDNESDAY 9

Venus square Uranus: another good day to be careful with conversations and communications, as you may be surprised by someone's viewpoints. You may need to review a circumstance. Moon enters Gemini.

THURSDAY 10

Mercury trine Jupiter: a much better day for communications and to make agreements, although if tension is in the air it could reignite unless you're careful. A trip could be ideal. Moon in Gemini.

FRIDAY 11 (

Moon enters Cancer.

SATURDAY 12 (

Sun trine Chiron: this is a healing day, and you can overcome hurdles with a compassionate, positive approach. It's a good day for health and beauty appointments. Moon in Cancer.

SUNDAY 13 (

Sun conjunct Venus; Venus semi-sextile Mars: a good day for talks and for beauty and health treats. Romance and the arts could also thrive. Moon in Cancer.

AUGUST

S	M	T	W	T	F	S
		1	2	3	4	5
6	7	8	10	10	11	12
13	14	15	16	17	18	19
20	21	22	23	24	25	26
27	28	29	30	31		

MONDAY 14 ☽

Moon enters Leo.

TUESDAY 15 ☽

Sun semi-sextile Mars; Mercury semi-sextile Venus: a good day to take action where in the past you have not trusted your own abilities. It's also a good time for a reunion and to catch up with an old friend. Moon in Leo.

WEDNESDAY 16 ○

New moon in Leo; Mercury quincunx Chiron; Mars trine Uranus: the Leo new moon asks that you embrace your ability to make things happen! This is a good day to do something different and enjoy the company of like-minded people. You may enjoy a spontaneous event but must avoid making rash decisions. A health matter may require attention.

THURSDAY 17 ☽

Moon in Virgo.

FRIDAY 18)

Moon in Virgo.

SATURDAY 19)

Moon enters Libra.

SUNDAY 20)

Sun quincunx Neptune: ensure you have all the details if you're making key decisions or you could make mistakes. Avoid being pressured into making decisions. Moon in Libra.

AUGUST

S	M	T	W	T	F	S
		1	2	3	4	5
6	7	8	10	10	11	12
13	14	15	16	17	18	19
20	21	22	23	24	25	26
27	28	29	30	31		

august to
september 2023

Sun enters Virgo, 23 August

Just as the sun enters Virgo, Mercury, the ruler of Virgo, will turn retrograde, suggesting the next four weeks will merit a careful and considered approach and especially for Virgos, Geminis, Pisceans and Sagittarians.

Furthermore, on 27 August the sun will align opposite Saturn from our point of view on earth, and this can spell a time when you must be serious and make considered decisions. This is a good time to research information that helps you to understand your circumstances better. Be reasonable and logical, and you will know just what to do.

At the same time energetic Mars will enter Libra, which could heighten a sense of indecision or insecurity. It will therefore be an ideal time to boost your nervous system with stress-busting habits such as exercise, meditation and communing with nature.

The Pisces full moon and supermoon on 31 August will point out for you where you could dream big, but with a word of caution: ensure you build your dreams on facts rather than supposition or you could allow your imagination to run away with you.

The first week of September will provide an optimistic interlude when socialising and networking will appeal. You could make great progress with your ventures at this time but you must avoid overestimating your reach. Be practical with your plans and they will succeed.

The new moon in Virgo on 15 September will be an ideal time to dream big but you must keep an eye on details. You could make momentous change at this new moon that will result in stability and security (even if there is a little upheaval in the process).

For Virgos

It's time to get real Virgo, and to focus on what – and who – truly matters for you. Find ways to extend your knowledge base and social circle as this will help you to make the changes this month that are necessary. As a result, you could set truly transformative change in motion. A little planning will go a long way.

The Pisces full moon and supermoon on 31 August signals the chance to revitalise your life, especially if it's your birthday on or before then. If you were born later in September, this supermoon points to an excellent time to turn a key corner at work or with a health situation.

The Virgo new moon on 15 September asks that your trust your imagination and allow your intuition and dreams to provide inspiration. You can make such a huge leap in changing your daily life – at work and in your projects and ventures, and for some in your financial and personal lives. Be prepared to live your dreams, but also to be practical as you build a secure future.

MONDAY 21 〉

Sun quincunx Pluto: you can make great progress but you must avoid power struggles. Moon in Libra.

TUESDAY 22 〉

Venus square Jupiter; Mars opposite Neptune: a good time to check details and that you are sticking to your principles. That said, you may need to state your case clearly and concisely or you could be pressured into something you don't want or could become part of a conflict. Moon in Scorpio.

WEDNESDAY 23 〉

Sun enters Virgo; Mercury turns retrograde: you may receive key news. It's time to be practical and focus over the next few weeks on your health, well-being, work, nurturance and support. Moon in Scorpio.

THURSDAY 24 〉

Moon enters Sagittarius.

FRIDAY 25 ●

Mars trine Pluto: this is a good time to steam ahead with your various projects and ventures. Be prepared to knuckle down and be serious about your goals. Moon in Sagittarius.

SATURDAY 26 ●

Moon enters Capricorn.

SUNDAY 27 ●

Mars enters Libra; sun opposite Saturn: serious decisions and commitments can be made now. If you feel your options are limited, look for brand new ways ahead. Moon in Capricorn.

AUGUST

S	M	T	W	T	F	S
		1	2	3	4	5
6	7	8	10	10	11	12
13	14	15	16	17	18	19
20	21	22	23	24	25	26
27	28	29	30	31		

MONDAY 28 ●

Moon enters Aquarius.

TUESDAY 29 ●

Moon in Aquarius.

WEDNESDAY 30 ●

Moon enters Pisces.

THURSDAY 31 ●

Full moon and supermoon in Pisces; Mercury quincunx Chiron: this is a good day to gain perspective and review important matters. It's also a good day for a health appointment or to seek expert help and to offer it, even if it seems challenging. Dream big, but also be practical.

FRIDAY 1 ●

Mars quincunx Saturn: a good time to be practical, even if you are reaching towards a goal or a dream. Avoid making rash decisions. Moon enters Aries.

SATURDAY 2 ●

Moon in Aries.

SUNDAY 3 ●

Moon enters Taurus.

	SEPTEMBER					
S	M	T	W	T	F	S
					1	2
3	4	5	6	7	8	9
10	11	12	13	14	15	16
17	18	19	20	21	22	23
24	25	26	27	28	29	30

MONDAY 4 ●

Venus ends its retrograde phase; Mercury trine Jupiter: a good time to evaluate how you wish your communications to flourish. A trip or meeting may need to be postponed, or you will revisit an old haunt. Plan ahead to avoid delays. Moon in Taurus.

TUESDAY 5 ●

Sun semi-sextile Venus: a good day for shopping, but watch you don't overspend! Romance and the arts will appeal. Moon enters Gemini.

WEDNESDAY 6 ◀

Sun conjunct Mercury: you're likely to hear key news to do with a trip or finances. A meeting will have a nostalgic feel to it. You may enjoy a return to an old haunt. Moon in Gemini.

THURSDAY 7 ◀

Mercury semi-sextile Venus: a good day for financial plans and to discuss your ideas with someone close, either at work or in your personal life. You'll enjoy socialising. Moon in Gemini.

FRIDAY 8 ☾

Sun trine Jupiter: a good time to socialise and network, and you may feel optimistic and positive. Key news or a meeting could be decisive. You may also be lucky or will embark on a journey. Moon in Cancer.

SATURDAY 9 ☾

Moon in Cancer.

SUNDAY 10 ☾

Moon enters Leo.

SEPTEMBER

S	M	T	W	T	F	S
					1	2
3	4	5	6	7	8	9
10	11	12	13	14	15	16
17	18	19	20	21	22	23
24	25	26	27	28	29	30

MONDAY 11   (

Mercury semi-sextile Mars: a good day to initiate talks and meetings. You may be inclined to be a little impulsive, though, so think things through. Moon in Leo.

TUESDAY 12   (

Moon in Leo.

WEDNESDAY 13   (

Moon enters Virgo.

THURSDAY 14   (

Moon in Virgo.

FRIDAY 15 ○

New moon in Virgo: take notice of developments as they will give you a heads-up about your future potential and how to attain a strong platform. Moon enters Libra.

SATURDAY 16 ⟩

Sun trine Uranus: you may receive unexpected news. Be adaptable to other people's ideas. Moon in Libra.

SUNDAY 17 ⟩

Venus square Jupiter: communications will merit a little care and attention to avoid making an already tense situation worse. Aim to listen to someone else's opinion even if you do not agree with it. Moon in Libra.

SEPTEMBER

S	M	T	W	T	F	S
					1	2
3	4	5	6	7	8	9
10	11	12	13	14	15	16
17	18	19	20	21	22	23
24	25	26	27	28	29	30

MONDAY 18 ☽

Moon in Scorpio.

TUESDAY 19 ☽

Sun opposite Neptune; Mars quincunx Jupiter: a meeting or news will be inspiring but may also be frustrating. Avoid delays and mix-ups by being super clear. Mistakes could be made, so before you make major decisions ensure you have the facts straight. Moon in Scorpio.

WEDNESDAY 20 ☽

Moon enters Sagittarius.

THURSDAY 21 ☽

Sun trine Pluto: considerable developments will mean a significant change. If you'd like to initiate change this is a positive time to test the waters. Be adventurous. Moon in Sagittarius.

FRIDAY 22

Moon enters Capricorn.

SATURDAY 23

Sun enters Libra: this is the autumn equinox, a time to integrate ideas, give thanks and prepare for winter. Look for balance and a fair go over the coming weeks and be practical. Moon in Capricorn.

SUNDAY 24

Mars opposite Chiron: a good time to be tactful and diplomatic and seek mutual respect from others. Avoid taking the opinions of others personally and look for solutions. An expert, teacher or adviser may be helpful and a health situation may require advice. Moon in Capricorn.

SEPTEMBER

S	M	T	W	T	F	S
					1	2
3	4	5	6	7	8	9
10	11	12	13	14	15	16
17	18	19	20	21	22	23
24	25	26	27	28	29	30

september to october 2023

Sun enters Libra, 23 September

As the sun enters Libra this is the autumn equinox, and as the seasons change it is a good time to seek greater harmony and balance in your home life as you may well be spending more time indoors.

Communications are likely to improve early in October, so if things have been a little tense a smoother path should begin to materialise then. Nevertheless, tact and diplomacy will be clever tools to use in early October as misunderstandings could still arise.

As you travel through October prepare for the second eclipse season of the year – and eclipse seasons can mean intense times. What's more, the square aspect between Mars and Pluto on 9 October could lead to fiery, explosive behaviour and the making of rash decisions around that time, so be mindful to avoid destroying what you have already built or you could regret your actions.

Once Mars enters Scorpio on 12 October passions ramp up and conflict is possible, so if you are already in a tense situation avoid stoking any fires. Be prepared instead to make solid, stable agreements. Luckily, the trine between Mars and Saturn will facilitate this on 13 October.

The annular solar eclipse on 14 October will be one to remember, not only for its beauty but also for its effects. It will bring old acquaintances into the foreground, and you'll need to keep those close to you in the loop about your plans. A health or work matter is best tackled carefully to avoid complications further down the line. The help of an expert or adviser may be super important and useful now.

For Librans

This zodiacal month is likely to be fairly intense. In early October you may tend to be a little perfectionist as your sign's ruler Venus enters Virgo, so aim to find the balance and peace you crave. The opposition of your sign's ruler Venus and Saturn on 10 October will be a good time to make a solid commitment to a reasonable course of action, but if you have been in conflict with someone you must avoid exacerbating already tense circumstances and thereby potentially limiting your options moving forward.

The annular solar eclipse in your sign on 14 October is a true turning point in your life. You may need to make a difficult decision or undertake a complex talk that has long-term consequences. A health or personal matter will demand that you use your famed tact and diplomacy and look for the peace you so proactively seek. This may be an intense decision, but the goals must be stability and security.

Circumstances will involve a return to an old haunt or a reunion. For some, though, there will be a parting of ways if you realise you cannot proceed on the same path.

MONDAY 25 ●

Sun quincunx Saturn; Mercury trine Jupiter: look for new solutions to old problems if an obstacle arises. Persevere with work and chores and you will attain your goals. A trip or meeting will appeal. Moon in Aquarius.

TUESDAY 26 ●

Moon in Aquarius.

WEDNESDAY 27 ●

Moon in Pisces.

THURSDAY 28 ●

Moon in Pisces.

FRIDAY 29 ●

Full moon in Aries: a good time to turn a corner in a relationship, commitment or agreement, but you must avoid making impulsive decisions.

SATURDAY 30 ●

Mercury semi-sextile Mars: a good time to be adventurous and proactive and meet new people. Moon in Aries.

SUNDAY 1 ●

Mercury semi-sextile Venus; Mars quincunx Uranus: you may experience a surprise or undergo a challenge, but rest assured you will gain ground and attain your goals. Avoid rash decisions as you are likely to regret them. This is a good time for get-togethers and to discuss plans and finances. You may enjoy a short trip or visit. Moon in Taurus.

SEPTEMBER

S	M	T	W	T	F	S
					1	2
3	4	5	6	7	8	9
10	11	12	13	14	15	16
17	18	19	20	21	22	23
24	25	26	27	28	29	30

MONDAY 2 ●

Mercury opposite Neptune: you'll enjoy a trip somewhere beautiful or a lovely get-together. However, you may tend to be idealistic or forgetful so keep an eye on details. Avoid delays by planning ahead. Moon in Taurus.

TUESDAY 3 ◐

Mercury trine Pluto: this is a good day for discussions, a short trip and planning long-term developments that could alter a relationship, work or finances. It's also a good time for gardening and improving your environment in general. Moon in Gemini.

WEDNESDAY 4 ◐

Venus quincunx Neptune: avoid idealism and be practical. Moon in Gemini.

THURSDAY 5 ◐

Mercury quincunx Saturn; Mars quincunx Neptune: keep an eye on your goals as you may be easily distracted. If you work towards an outcome you may experience a financial or work improvement. Moon enters Cancer.

FRIDAY 6 ◖

Venus quincunx Pluto: your ideas and values may differ from someone else's, but this needn't cause a fallout if you care for them. Moon in Cancer.

SATURDAY 7 ◖

Sun quincunx Jupiter: you'll find ways to overcome a hurdle. If you have argued with someone you may need to agree to disagree. Moon in Cancer.

SUNDAY 8 ◖

Moon in Leo.

OCTOBER

S	M	T	W	T	F	S
1	2	3	4	5	6	7
8	9	10	11	12	13	14
15	16	17	18	19	20	21
22	23	24	25	26	27	28
29	30	31				

MONDAY 9 ❨

Venus enters Virgo; Mars square Pluto: you may experience tension and arguments, so take time out if you feel under pressure. Find ways to unwind and destress and avoid unrealistic expectations and a perfectionist attitude in your personal life. Moon in Leo.

TUESDAY 10 ❨

Venus opposite Saturn: this is a good time to look for balance, otherwise antagonistic feelings could arise. It's also a good time to make an agreement or commitment even if it represents a hurdle. Moon enters Virgo.

WEDNESDAY 11 ❨

Sun opposite Chiron: if you feel vulnerable take short breaks. It's a good day for a health and well-being check. Someone may need your help or you may need someone's help; it will be available. Moon in Virgo.

THURSDAY 12 ❨

Mars enters Scorpio; Mercury quincunx Jupiter: you will feel passionate but you must be prepared to be flexible and adaptable, especially with travel and financial matters. However, if you are convinced you are correct you can attain your goals. Moon in Virgo.

FRIDAY 13   ☾

Mars trine Saturn: a good day to follow your passions and invest in people and ideas. It's also a good day to get things done. You could make a solid agreement or commitment; just avoid making rash decisions. Moon in Libra.

SATURDAY 14   ○

Annular solar eclipse in Libra; Mercury opposite Chiron: expect a reunion or news from the past. Be tactful to avoid conflict if intense talks arise. Some health matters may be delicate. Some relationships may experience a deeper commitment and others a parting of ways.

SUNDAY 15   ☽

Sun quincunx Uranus: you may undergo an unexpected or unusual experience. You will attain your goals by being diligent. Moon enters Scorpio.

OCTOBER

S	M	T	W	T	F	S
1	2	3	4	5	6	7
8	9	10	11	12	13	14
15	16	17	18	19	20	21
22	23	24	25	26	27	28
29	30	31				

MONDAY 16   )

Moon in Scorpio.

TUESDAY 17   )

Mercury quincunx Uranus: you may hear unexpected news or must undergo a difficult or complex transaction. Keep conversations on an even keel. Avoid impulsiveness. Travel and communications may be delayed or complex. Moon enters Sagittarius.

WEDNESDAY 18   )

Moon in Sagittarius.

THURSDAY 19   )

Sun quincunx Neptune; Mercury conjunct moon's south node: you'll enjoy a return to an old haunt, or you may hear from an old friend or acquaintance. You may be idealistic or forgetful, so be practical to avoid mistakes. Moon in Sagittarius.

FRIDAY 20 ☽

Sun conjunct Mercury: key news or a meeting will be significant. Avoid arguments if tension arises, as these are likely to escalate quickly. Moon in Capricorn.

SATURDAY 21 ☽

Sun and Mercury square Pluto: a meeting or news may be intense. Find ways to de-stress and unwind when you can. You could accomplish a great deal, but you must be focused and avoid taking on other people's problems while also being compassionate. Moon in Capricorn.

SUNDAY 22 ☽

Mercury enters Scorpio; Mercury trine Saturn; Venus trine Jupiter: you may feel more outgoing and drawn to make life more interesting and enjoyable. You'll get chores done and make constructive decisions and commitments by avoiding stubbornness both in yourself and others. Moon enters Aquarius.

OCTOBER

S	M	T	W	T	F	S
1	2	3	4	5	6	7
8	9	10	11	12	13	14
15	16	17	18	19	20	21
22	23	24	25	26	27	28
29	30	31				

october to
november 2023

Sun enters Scorpio, 23 October

As the sun enters passionate Scorpio it joins Mercury and Mars, all in a favourable trine aspect with Saturn. This points to the chance over the coming four weeks to build a solid platform for yourself and those you love, but you will need to be prepared to do something different and to seek inspiration. Mercury in Scorpio and subsequently Sagittarius will facilitate research and a deeper understanding of your circumstances. The grand trine between Uranus, Venus and Pluto at the end of October and early November will offer ample opportunity to transform your life if this is what you want.

However, the intensity of the partial lunar eclipse in Taurus on 28 October is not to be underestimated. If you are a fixed sign (Taurus, Scorpio, Aquarius or Leo) you may find this a tough interlude, as you tend to avoid change on a grand scale unless absolutely necessary. That said, when you do embrace change you're particularly good at it!

For all zodiac signs this month and the next are ideal for engaging the transformations in your life you have been planning for a while that are long term. The growing trine between Uranus and Pluto will facilitate your plans but, again, it's important to be practical or these times could prove to be confusing or plain overwhelming.

The entry of Venus into its own sign Libra on 8 November spells a time when luxury and self-indulgence will appeal, and there will be a strong draw to the arts, romance and good food and drink.

For Scorpios

The partial lunar eclipse in Taurus on 28 October points to the beginning of a significant new cycle in your personal life, especially if it's your birthday on that date.

This will be an intense time but also one when transformations can occur. It's a good time to find new avenues for self-expression, both at work and at play. The key to finding more stability lies in being inspired by your need for security and to consciously create it both for yourself and those you love. It's possible now.

The entrance of Venus into Libra on 8 November points to increasing enjoyment of life, and you may be particularly drawn to expressing your deepest desires. You may enjoy a secret or passionate love affair or meet an alluring and influential character.

The Scorpio new moon on 13 November points to the chance to break out of a tired routine. If you have been avoiding making difficult decisions, events around this new moon may decide them for you. Expect an out-of-the-ordinary development. As you move forward in November keep an eye on what is reasonable and avoid allowing your expectations to exceed the realities, then you could truly excel. If you're looking for romance, 17 November could be an ideal date!

MONDAY 23

Sun enters Scorpio: this spells a passionate, upbeat and potentially intense four weeks. Be prepared to channel your energy into work and building strong and secure foundations. Moon in Aquarius.

TUESDAY 24

Sun trine Saturn: a good day to make agreements and commitments. You may experience a financial improvement. Moon enters Pisces.

WEDNESDAY 25

Moon in Pisces.

THURSDAY 26

Moon enters Aries.

FRIDAY 27 ●

Moon in Aries.

SATURDAY 28 ●

Partial lunar eclipse in Taurus; Mars opposite Jupiter: this is an important decision-making time. Ensure you are careful with your plans and avoid making rash decisions. A trip or meeting could signal a fresh chapter.

SUNDAY 29 ●

Mercury conjunct Mars; Mercury opposite Jupiter: a trip or meeting will bring your passionate side out but it may also bring out obstinacy, both in yourself and others. If you're engaged in conflict it is likely to escalate, so be careful. Avoid making rash decisions. Moon in Taurus.

OCTOBER

S	M	T	W	T	F	S
1	2	3	4	5	6	7
8	9	10	11	12	13	14
15	16	17	18	19	20	21
22	23	24	25	26	27	28
29	30	31				

MONDAY 30 ●

Moon enters Gemini.

TUESDAY 31 ●

Venus trine Uranus: happy Hallowe'en! This is always a quirky day, and this year it will be different again; you may enjoy it more than usual. You're likely to experience a few unexpected surprises and will feel sociable and spontaneous. Moon in Gemini.

WEDNESDAY 1 ●

Moon enters Cancer.

THURSDAY 2 ●

Moon in Cancer.

FRIDAY 3

Sun opposite Jupiter; Venus opposite Neptune: you're likely to view the world as being larger than life and may be easily influenced. Find balance if you feel you're being overwhelmed. It's a good day to get together with friends and for romance, but you must avoid overindulgence as you'll regret it! Moon in Cancer.

SATURDAY 4

Mercury opposite Uranus: you may encounter an out-of-the-ordinary circumstance or hear unusual news. You may bump into an old friend. Moon enters Leo.

SUNDAY 5

Mars quincunx Chiron: be careful with your movements to avoid minor bumps and scrapes. Avoid impulsiveness. Someone may ask for help, and if you need it then help will be available. Moon in Leo.

NOVEMBER

S	M	T	W	T	F	S
			1	2	3	4
5	6	7	8	9	10	11
12	13	14	15	16	17	18
19	20	21	22	23	24	25
26	27	28	29	30		

MONDAY 6 ☾

Venus trine Pluto: you'll enjoy a meeting or get-together. If you'd like to make long-term changes this is a good time to do so. Moon enters Virgo.

TUESDAY 7 ☾

Mercury trine Neptune: a good time for talks and meetings. You may travel somewhere beautiful or near water. Romance will appeal. You may be easily influenced, so if you are making financial decisions do your research. Moon in Virgo.

WEDNESDAY 8 ☾

Venus enters Libra; Venus quincunx Saturn: the arts, romance and fair play will all appeal increasingly over the coming weeks. You may be drawn to update your wardrobe or looks. You will overcome a hurdle through hard work and diligence. Moon in Virgo.

THURSDAY 9 ☾

Sun quincunx Chiron; Mercury sextile Pluto: a talk or meeting could be transformative, so take the initiative if you want to meet someone or make changes. It's a good day for health talks and for getting expert advice, even if obstacles initially arise. Moon enters Libra.

FRIDAY 10   (

Mercury enters Sagittarius; Mercury square Saturn: you will be feeling adventurous and outgoing but some communications may be tense, so avoid arguments and instead find common ground. Look for fair play and balance. Moon in Libra.

SATURDAY 11   (

Mars opposite Uranus: developments may come about unexpectedly. You'll enjoy being spontaneous but must avoid making rash decisions. Avoid minor bumps and scrapes. Moon enters Scorpio.

SUNDAY 12   (

Moon in Scorpio.

NOVEMBER

S	M	T	W	T	F	S
			1	2	3	4
5	6	7	8	9	10	11
12	13	14	15	16	17	18
19	20	21	22	23	24	25
26	27	28	29	30		

MONDAY 13 ○

New moon in Scorpio; sun opposite Uranus: this will be a passionate and potentially intense new moon, and it will entail a surprise! You may bump into someone or hear from someone unexpectedly.

TUESDAY 14 ☽

Moon enters Sagittarius.

WEDNESDAY 15 ☽

Mercury sextile Venus: a good day for meetings, a trip and financial arrangements. Shopping may appeal. You may be feeling super generous so avoid overspending, especially if you're in debt. Moon in Sagittarius.

THURSDAY 16 ☽

Mercury and Venus quincunx Jupiter: you will overcome obstacles but you need to choose your words carefully. Travel may be delayed, so plan ahead. Keep expectations realistic and you could move mountains. Moon in Capricorn.

FRIDAY 17 〉

Sun and Mars trine Neptune: keep your dreams alive and you could make some of them come true, especially if you carried out adequate research earlier this month and year. Romance could blossom, so make a date! Moon in Capricorn.

SATURDAY 18 〉

Sun conjunct Mars: this is likely to be an active weekend, and you'll enjoy the arts, music, romance, film and dance. If you're spiritually minded this is a good time to expand your interests. Avoid making snap decisions. Moon enters Aquarius.

SUNDAY 19 〉

Moon in Aquarius.

NOVEMBER

S	M	T	W	T	F	S
			1	2	3	4
5	6	7	8	9	10	11
12	13	14	15	16	17	18
19	20	21	22	23	24	25
26	27	28	29	30		

MONDAY 20 ☽

Sun sextile Pluto: a good time for making long-range changes and deepening your relationships and interest in projects. Moon enters Pisces.

TUESDAY 21 ☽

Moon in Pisces.

WEDNESDAY 22 ☽

Sun enters Sagittarius; Venus opposite Chiron: let your inner adventurer out over the coming weeks, but be careful to also be realistic. Someone may need your help or you may need someone's help. It's a good day for a beauty or health appointment. Moon enters Aries.

THURSDAY 23 ☽

Sun square Saturn: a good day to focus on chores and work, and being a little more adventurous than usual — without overdoing it! Rules and limitations will play a role in decisions you make now. Moon in Aries.

FRIDAY 24 ●

Mars enters Sagittarius; Mercury quincunx Uranus: you may receive out-of-the-ordinary news or will need to leave your comfort zone. Avoid making snap decisions. Plan ahead to avoid traffic delays and mix-ups. Moon enters Taurus.

SATURDAY 25 ●

Mars square Saturn: you may need to rethink your plans. Avoid feeling frustrated and find constructive ways to dissipate excess energy. If you make constructive plans you could progress with projects, but you must be patient. Moon in Taurus.

SUNDAY 26 ●

Venus quincunx Uranus: be prepared to view matters from someone else's point of view. You may be surprised by developments. Moon in Taurus.

NOVEMBER

S	M	T	W	T	F	S
			1	2	3	4
5	6	7	8	9	10	11
12	13	14	15	16	17	18
19	20	21	22	23	24	25
26	27	28	29	30		

November to December 2023

Sun enters Sagittarius, 22 November

Just as the sun enters Sagittarius it squares Saturn, suggesting this month your hard work will be rewarded – but it will be hard work! At the same time Venus will oppose Chiron, which suggests personal circumstances may require delicate handling. If you experience a disagreement or fallout with someone at this time, take time out to re-evaluate where you stand.

This is a good time to seek professional and expert advice if you feel you're unable to work constructively with any prevailing circumstances that are outside your control. It's a time to avoid taking other people's situations personally and to be ready to help them and ask for help yourself if it's needed.

The entry of Mars into Sagittarius on 24 November will add to a sense of urgency and also potentially to a sense of frustration if you don't get your way now, so find ways to dissipate restless energy otherwise you may feel antagonistic.

Luckily, when Mercury enters earthy Capricorn in early December some of the rushed atmosphere and pressure will dissipate, although when Venus enters Scorpio a few days later passions and ego battles are likely to arise with more frequency. Find time now to engage your stress-busting skill sets such as regular exercise.

For Sagittarians

Mars will enter your sign shortly after the sun, bringing an additional boost of energy. You will feel a call to the wild and to adventure. However, because both the sun and Mars will square Saturn your need to expand your horizons may well be limited or you will feel restricted by other people's rules and regulations or boundaries. This will be a good time to plan ahead and be patient, otherwise a sense of frustration or anger will set in.

The Gemini full moon on 27 November will kick-start a fresh chapter, in your personal life if you were born on or before this date and in your work, health or daily schedule if you were born later. Keep communications super clear to avoid making mistakes.

Luckily, Mercury's transit into Capricorn on 1 December will help you to formulate practical and realistic plans and at least to discuss them. Just avoid ego battles early in December as these could derail your best-laid plans.

The Sagittarian new moon on 12 December will encourage you to turn a corner, but you may need to be careful to avoid hurting someone's feelings as you do so. There is a degree of the unpredictable around this new moon, so be careful not to step on anyone's toes or even to score a home goal if you are tempted by rash behaviour.

Try to get important paperwork and decisions finalised before 13 December, unless you wish to review them over the coming months. The Mars–Chiron trine on 15 December will reveal whether your plans will withstand obstacles or if you have acted rashly.

MONDAY 27 ●

Full moon in Gemini; Mercury square Neptune; Mercury trine moon's north node: there is a sense of the inevitable as some matters will simply be out of your control, so good communication skills will be useful. A meeting or news will be significant. Avoid misunderstandings and travel delays by planning ahead.

TUESDAY 28 ●

Moon in Gemini.

WEDNESDAY 29 ●

Sun quincunx Jupiter: a good day to discuss your plans, but avoid feeling they can be achieved super quickly. A travel or legal matter may need to be reconsidered. You will overcome obstacles through diligence. Moon in Cancer.

THURSDAY 30 ●

Mercury semi-sextile Pluto; Venus quincunx Neptune: a good time for get-togethers and romance and for discussing long-term changes. Just ensure you have the facts straight and that you're on the same page. Moon in Cancer.

FRIDAY 1 ●

Mercury enters Capricorn: communications are likely to become a little less rushed over the coming weeks, but you must avoid stubbornness in yourself and others. Moon enters Leo.

SATURDAY 2 ●

Mercury sextile Saturn: a good day for making arrangements and commitments to a plan, person or project. Moon in Leo.

SUNDAY 3 ●

Venus square Pluto; Mars quincunx Jupiter: this may be an intense day. You may not agree with someone else's actions and ideas. Avoid a battle of egos, as it's likely to escalate. Research facts rather than follow destructive emotions. Moon in Leo.

DECEMBER

S	M	T	W	T	F	S
					1	2
3	4	5	6	7	8	9
10	11	12	13	14	15	16
17	18	19	20	21	22	23
24	25	26	27	28	29	30
31						

MONDAY 4 ◖

Venus enters Scorpio: over the next few weeks you'll be drawn to express your desires and values more passionately, and so will everyone else! Avoid conflict and look for healthy ways to channel excess energy into fab ventures. Moon in Virgo.

TUESDAY 5 ◖

Venus trine Saturn: a good day for discussions and meetings and for financial decisions. If you have recently argued it's a good day to build bridges. It's also a good day for a beauty treat or improving your wardrobe. Moon in Virgo.

WEDNESDAY 6 ◖

Moon enters Libra.

THURSDAY 7 ◖

Moon in Libra.

FRIDAY 8 (

Sun trine Chiron; Mercury trine Jupiter: a good day for a health and beauty treat, and for meeting and talking to experts and advisers who can be helpful. A financial, personal or travel matter could move forward. Moon in Libra.

SATURDAY 9 (

Moon in Scorpio.

SUNDAY 10 (

Venus opposite Jupiter: a good day for meetings and talks and for focusing on the people and activities most important to you. Avoid arguments, as they could get out of hand. A reunion will be poignant. Moon in Scorpio.

DECEMBER

S	M	T	W	T	F	S
					1	2
3	4	5	6	7	8	9
10	11	12	13	14	15	16
17	18	19	20	21	22	23
24	25	26	27	28	29	30
31						

MONDAY 11   (

Mercury sextile Venus: a good day for get-togethers and a trip. It's also a good day to sort out finances. Romance could flourish. Moon enters Sagittarius.

TUESDAY 12   ○

New moon in Sagittarius; sun quincunx Uranus: a good time to be adventurous with your plans and ideas. Just be sure to keep all those you love in the loop. Someone may be feeling vulnerable now, and if it's you you'll find the help and support you need. You may be surprised by events.

WEDNESDAY 13   )

Mercury turns retrograde: you may receive key news and will get the chance to quietly review your options and ideas over the coming few weeks. Moon enters Capricorn.

THURSDAY 14   )

Moon in Capricorn.

FRIDAY 15 ⟩

Mars trine Chiron: a good day to focus on health and well-being. If you are indulging in seasonal celebrations avoid over-indulging as you'll regret it! Someone may need your help or you may need someone's help; if so, it will be available. Moon enters Aquarius.

SATURDAY 16 ⟩

Moon in Aquarius.

SUNDAY 17 ⟩

Sun square Neptune; Venus quincunx Chiron: if you feel a little under the weather or sensitive and vulnerable, avoid taking other people's opinions personally. You may be prone to misplacing valuables, so keep an eye on your keys. Moon enters Pisces.

DECEMBER

S	M	T	W	T	F	S
					1	2
3	4	5	6	7	8	9
10	11	12	13	14	15	16
17	18	19	20	21	22	23
24	25	26	27	28	29	30
31						

MONDAY 18

Mercury trine Jupiter: a good day for get-togethers and important talks and meetings that may relate back to circumstances earlier in December. A trip or reunion is on the cards. Moon in Pisces.

TUESDAY 19

Moon enters Aries.

WEDNESDAY 20

Venus semi-sextile Mars: this is a good day to feel optimistic about your ventures and projects and be proactive, but avoid grandiose gestures and risk taking. Moon in Aries.

THURSDAY 21

Sun semi-sextile Pluto; Venus opposite Uranus; Mars quincunx Uranus: you may enjoy a surprise or unusual event, although there will be an element of spontaneity that could be embraced. Be prepared to exit your comfort zone — within reason! Moon in Aries.

FRIDAY 22

Sun enters Capricorn; sun conjunct Mercury: thoughts may turn to the practicalities of the holiday season and to the new year of 2024. News from the past will be significant. Avoid travel delays by planning ahead. Moon in Taurus.

SATURDAY 23

Mercury semi-sextile Pluto: you'll enjoy a reunion and deepening your understanding of someone. A trip could be transformative. Moon in Taurus.

SUNDAY 24

Sun sextile Saturn: this is a good time to create stability and security. A meeting with a father or authority figure will be significant. Moon enters Gemini.

DECEMBER

S	M	T	W	T	F	S
					1	2
3	4	5	6	7	8	9
10	11	12	13	14	15	16
17	18	19	20	21	22	23
24	25	26	27	28	29	30
31						

December 2023

Sun enters Capricorn, 22 December

As the sun steps into Capricorn, this marks the winter solstice in the northern hemisphere, a time when we collectively reflect on the hard work we have done all year and prepare to plant new seeds of hope for the coming year.

There is a strong flavour of the past with reunions and returns to old haunts as there usually is at this time of year, but perhaps more so this year than in previous years. You'll appreciate the chance to catch up with old friends and family, which will provide a sense of stability and security.

However, there is also simultaneously a sense of potential loss at this time. Avoid feeling nostalgic if you are missing someone. Look for ways to connect with people in an upbeat, optimistic way and especially at Christmas, as you will enjoy unexpected developments that make your heart soar.

A word of warning: these are exuberant stars this year in the seasonal phase, so avoid extravagance you can't afford or overindulgence that leaves you feeling unwell. Maintain a sense of proportion if you can!

There is much to be happy about, and if you love the end-of-year sales you may be tempted to overspend. Just keep an eye on your budget. Happy New Year!

For more about Capricorn in January 2024 reserve your copy of the *2024 Astrology Diary*; see Rockpool Publishing at: www.rockpoolpublishing.com and www.patsybennett.com.

Wishing everyone a very happy solstice, Yuletide and New Year!

For Capricorns

Just as the sun enters your sign it conjuncts retrograde Mercury, suggesting important reunions and news that you must carefully process. Mercury is retrograde in your 12th house, suggesting you'll feel you are going over old ground either physically through reunions or mentally via nostalgia. Take a moment to assess how to maximise a sense of optimism at this time, as you may be prone to negative thinking.

Luckily, a positive aspect with family and friends will get you out of a maudlin phase and bring a sense of celebration to the table. Christmas Day brings an especially romantic and creative atmosphere into your life, and you'll enjoy a boost in self-esteem.

The full moon in Cancer on 27 December suggests you are turning a corner in a key relationship, especially if it's your birthday on that date. For some this will be at work and for others in your personal life and health. Be financially constructive and proactive and you could truly begin an abundant phase, but you must avoid both financial and emotional gambling.

MONDAY 25 ●

Merry Christmas! Venus trine Neptune: there is a lovely romantic vibe this Christmas Day. You'll enjoy music and dance and being creative. The drawback? You may be tempted to overconsume, which you'll regret tomorrow! Moon in Gemini.

TUESDAY 26 ●

Mercury semi-sextile Venus: a good day for reunions, talks and meetings and also for shopping, as a little retail therapy may be enjoyable. You may be prone to overspend so avoid splurging, especially if you're already in debt. You'll enjoy an ego boost and possibly also a financial boost. Moon enters Cancer.

WEDNESDAY 27 ●

Full moon in Cancer; sun trine Jupiter; Mercury square Neptune: a lovely time to nurture yourself and others. Avoid misunderstandings and making decisions unless you have all the facts. A trip will be enjoyable but you must avoid traffic delays by planning ahead.

THURSDAY 28 ●

Mercury conjunct Mars; Mars square Neptune: a good day for meetings, talks and romance, but you must think before you speak or you will regret your indiscretions. You may be inclined to be extravagant and overindulge, so be careful! Moon in Cancer.

FRIDAY 29

Venus enters Sagittarius; Venus sextile Pluto: this is an expansive time when you'll feel more inclined to take risks, so while romance could flourish and you'll enjoy meetings and being outgoing, under these stars you must avoid speculation. Moon in Leo.

SATURDAY 30

Moon in Leo.

SUNDAY 31

Happy New Year! Moon enters Virgo.

DECEMBER

S	M	T	W	T	F	S
					1	2
3	4	5	6	7	8	9
10	11	12	13	14	15	16
17	18	19	20	21	22	23
24	25	26	27	28	29	30
31						

NOTES

NOTES

About the author

Patsy Bennett is a rare combination of astrologer and psychic medium. Her horoscopes are published in newspapers and magazines in Australia and internationally and she has written freelance for publications including *Nature and Health* and *Practical Parenting*. She has appeared on several live daytime TV and radio shows, including Studio 10 and The Project. Her books *Sun Sign Secrets*; *Astrology: Secrets of the Moon*, *2022 Horoscopes*, the *Astrology Diaries* and *Zodiac Moon Reading Cards* are published by Rockpool Publishing.

Born in New Zealand, Patsy relocated to the UK where, in the 1980s, she worked as a sub-editor and production editor for women's and fashion magazines including *Woman's Own* and *ELLE* (UK). She studied astrology at the Faculty of Astrological Studies in London in the 1990s and in 1998 she relocated to Australia, where she worked as a reporter for local newspapers in the northern New South Wales area, wrote freelance for magazines and continued her practice as an astrologer.

Patsy has worked as a professional astrologer and medium for 25 years. She began reading palms and tarot at the age of 14, and experienced mediumistic insights as young as 12. She is a natural medium and has perfected her skill by studying with some of the world's most experienced and foremost mediums. She provides astrology and psychic intuitive consultations and facilitates astrology and psychic development workshops in northern New South Wales and on the Gold Coast in Queensland.

Patsy gained a Master of Arts degree in Romance Languages and Literature at the University of London and taught at the University of California, Berkeley. She is a member of the Queensland Federation of Astrologers and the Spiritualists' National Union.

Patsy runs www.astrocast.com.au, www.patsybennett.com, facebook @patsybennettpsychicastrology and insta @patsybennettastrology.

Further reading of astronomical data

The American Ephemeris for the 21st Century 2000–2050 at Midnight, Michelsen, ACS Publications, 2010.

Computer programs of astronomical data

Solar Fire, Esoteric Technologies Pty Ltd.

Also by patsy Bennett

Sun Sign Secrets
Celestial guidance with the sun, moon and stars

ISBN: 9781925946352

This comprehensive, ground-breaking astrology book is for everyone who wants to make the most of their true potential and be in the flow with solar and lunar phases. It includes analyses of each sun sign from Aries to Pisces and pinpoints how you can dynamically make the most of your life in real time alongside celestial events. Work with the gifts and strengths of your sun sign in relation to every lunar phase, zodiacal month, new moon, full moon and eclipse.

Look up your sun sign to read all about your talents and potential pitfalls, and discover how to express your inner star power during the various phases of the sun and moon throughout the days, months and years to come.

Available at all good bookstores.

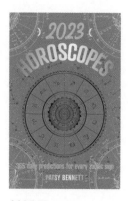

2023 Horoscopes
365 daily predictions for every zodiac sign

ISBN: 9781925946352

This is the only horoscope book you'll need next year! This complete astrological guide contains inspiring and motivational forecasts for 2023 so you can be well prepared for the year ahead. You will discover how to best navigate your opportunities and reach your full potential.

2023 Daily Horoscopes features daily horoscope predictions for all signs which explains what you can expect and the ideals days to attract wealth, love, success, and more. Plus, this book also includes a yearly overview of your love life, money, home life, career and health.

Available at all good bookstores.